Why Delegate?

Why Delegate?

Neil J. Mitchell

OXFORD
UNIVERSITY PRESS

OXFORD
UNIVERSITY PRESS

Oxford University Press is a department of the University of Oxford. It furthers
the University's objective of excellence in research, scholarship, and education
by publishing worldwide. Oxford is a registered trade mark of Oxford University
Press in the UK and certain other countries.

Published in the United States of America by Oxford University Press
198 Madison Avenue, New York, NY 10016, United States of America.

Library of Congress Cataloging-in-Publication Data
Names: Mitchell, Neil J. (Neil James), 1953– author.
Title: Why delegate? / Neil J. Mitchell.
Description: New York, NY : Oxford University Press, [2021] |
Includes bibliographical references and index.
Identifiers: LCCN 2020048320 (print) | LCCN 2020048321 (ebook) |
ISBN 9780190904197 (hardback) | ISBN 9780190904203 (paperback) |
ISBN 9780190904227 (epub)
Subjects: LCSH: Delegation of authority.
Classification: LCC HD50 .M58 2021 (print) | LCC HD50 (ebook) |
DDC 658.4/02—dc23
LC record available at https://lccn.loc.gov/2020048320
LC ebook record available at https://lccn.loc.gov/2020048321

DOI: 10.1093/oso/9780190904197.001.0001

For Renée

Contents

Contents

Acknowledgments

Getting someone else to do something for you is not easy, as I describe at some length in this book. But doing things on one's own is not easy either. Beyond building on the work of economists and political scientists in developing the arguments and illustrations in this book, I have had all sorts of help from coauthors, colleagues, and students. I began thinking about delegation issues in researching violations of human rights and sorting out the motives of the leaders and the led. Some of what is here and notably the opportunism of the principal in delegating or tolerating the wrongdoing of the agent was initially explored in *Agents of Atrocity* (2004) and *Democracy's Blameless Leaders* (2012). In trying to isolate the leader's and the agent's contributions to violations, I worked on the issues of human rights, sexual violence and agent-centered violations first with James M. McCormick at Iowa State University, then with Chris Butler, Tali Gluch, Alok Bohara, and Mani Nepal at the University of New Mexico. To better understand the agent's contributions to violations I became interested in the role of informal armed militias and vigilantes, teaming up with Sabine Carey, Mannheim University, to construct a database on these organizations. We wanted to find out what sorts of armed groups are out there, why governments outsource to these organizations, and with what consequences. That work continues. More recently, with Kristin Bakke and Dominic Perera (University College London) and Hannah Smidt (University of Zurich), I have been working on a project on civil society monitoring and how and why governments restrict civil society organizations to defeat fire-alarm monitoring. These collaborative projects also inform the argument and analysis presented in this book. At UCL I have been lucky enough to find not just good students but coauthors and generous colleagues. In afternoons spent in the Norfolk Arms, the Conflict and Change group have given comments on drafts of various chapters. Thanks in particular to Rod Abouharb, Kristin Bakke, Zeynep Bulutgil, Kate Cronin-Furman, Niheer Disandi, Sam Erkiletian, Thomas Gift, Jennifer Hodge, Andreas Juon, Nils Metternich, Jon Monten, Dominic Perera, Kit Rickard, Tatjana Stankovic, Katerina Tertytchnaya, Manuel Vogt, and Sigrid Weber. Thanks also to Tom Dannenbaum, now of the Fletcher School, for his comments on my treatment of war crimes. Some of the examples used in the book have been tried out in the classroom with UCL students. A special thanks goes to Eric Fair, who graciously agreed to speak with me about his experience as an American interrogator in Iraq. For suggesting this project, for a newfound interest in the National Football League, and for such thoughtful advice on how to structure the book, thanks to David Pervin and to Macey Fairchild of Oxford University Press and to my current editor, James Cook, for seeking out such useful reviews and for his ongoing encouragement. Many thanks to the anonymous reviewers who challenged me to firm up the arguments and the contribution. Renée Danziger encouraged me to take on the project and has seen and commented on multiple drafts. I am lucky to have her insights and most of all her love. Finally, thanks to my children, Colin and Kate, and sisters, Alison and Laura, for their love and support.

Why Delegate?

OXFORD
UNIVERSITY PRESS

Oxford University Press is a department of the University of Oxford. It furthers
the University's objective of excellence in research, scholarship, and education
by publishing worldwide. Oxford is a registered trade mark of Oxford University
Press in the UK and certain other countries.

Published in the United States of America by Oxford University Press
198 Madison Avenue, New York, NY 10016, United States of America.

Library of Congress Cataloging-in-Publication Data
Names: Mitchell, Neil J. (Neil James), 1953– author.
Title: Why delegate? / Neil J. Mitchell.
Description: New York, NY : Oxford University Press, [2021] |
Includes bibliographical references and index.
Identifiers: LCCN 2020048320 (print) | LCCN 2020048321 (ebook) |
ISBN 9780190904197 (hardback) | ISBN 9780190904203 (paperback) |
ISBN 9780190904227 (epub)
Subjects: LCSH: Delegation of authority.
Classification: LCC HD50 .M58 2021 (print) | LCC HD50 (ebook) |
DDC 658.4/02—dc23
LC record available at https://lccn.loc.gov/2020048320
LC ebook record available at https://lccn.loc.gov/2020048321

DOI: 10.1093/oso/9780190904197.001.0001

Hardback printed by Bridgeport National Bindery, Inc., United States of America

While the City denied using quotas, the settlement required it to notify all officers that ticket quotas were not police department policy.[2] It was an expensive lesson in the difficulties of delegating. As those in charge cannot observe the effort of the officer on the beat, the number of summonses indicated productivity. Of course, the community wants officers to work rather than shirk. But they do not want motion-going officers and just "numbers." The community did not benefit from this productivity. As we go up the chain of delegation from the officer on the beat to the mayor, who in turn answered to the community, nobody really benefited. Taxpayers were out of pocket to no purpose. Even the police officers who met their "numbers" were deprived of meaningful work, which is thought to be an important part of what makes us happy.

It is not easy to keep others on task, whether it is policing the Bronx, guarding the safety of the nation, or just fixing your car. As mayor of New York, as a political leader facing a security threat, or as a car owner, delegation brings with it an underlying anxiety. Who is really in control? Is the police officer going through the motions? Is your security official selling you out? Is the mechanic installing an unnecessary part?

The world turns on the delegation relationship and on one party authorizing another to do a task. Social, economic, and political life is inconceivable without it. It has a profound impact on us all, from mundane domestic interactions, to the running of a country or the international community, and from our recreational enjoyments to our spiritual life. *Why Delegate?* investigates the diverse and sometimes questionable mix of incentives we have for delegating in the first place, and then the difficult choices of why we select one agent over another, why we delegate one task rather than another, or why we sometimes continue to delegate to untrustworthy and opportunistic individuals. Large organizations cannot exist without delegation. Parceling out tasks to contractors, employees, or elected

---

[2] "New York City to Pay Up to $75 Million over Dismissed Summonses," *New York Times*, January 23, 2017. https://www.nytimes.com/2017/01/23/nyregion/new-york-city-agrees-to-settlement-over-summonses-that-were-dismissed.html.

representatives is essential for efficient production, democracy in large communities, and just to get us through the day. There seem to be few tasks too precious for us as individuals or as decision-makers in large organizations to leave to others.

There is the story told by the journalist and speechwriter James Fallows that President Jimmy Carter took it upon himself to manage the scheduling of the White House tennis court. He was a busy man, with Middle East peace to negotiate and hostage crises to settle. There were presumably others with the time and skill to sort out the order of play, but the president wanted to control the court. Tennis aside, even the most intimate matters may be delegated. Lovers may be matched and mothers surrogated. Ethical as well as intimacy boundaries to delegation are porous. We expect students to take their own tests and write their own papers, which does not prevent others from offering to perform these services for them. Delegation is part of the human condition, as are the difficult choices it brings with it. Its upside can be efficiency, shared responsibility, and even happiness; its downside can be conflict, corruption, and the attenuation of morals.

1

There is an underlying structure to delegation relationships. Economists offer the insights of principal-agent theory, where the principal contracts with an agent to accomplish a task. The principal and the agent are assumed to have conflicting goals. The agent may be in a position to act in a self-interested and surreptitious way at the expense of the principal. The car owner principal wants a road-worthy car or, perhaps, with a prospective buyer in mind, a paper trail showing that the owner is telling the truth and the car has been well looked after. The mechanic, on the other hand, may be tempted to pad the bill. For successful delegation, and we look at this relationship from the principal's perspective, the challenge is to keep control of the agent and to achieve an outcome in line with her interests. The amount of control exercised by the principal depends on the amount of task-related and agent-related information the principal possesses. Conventionally, the person in charge is at a disadvantage and lacks information about the agent's qualities and about what he is actually doing.

Principals and agents might be individuals like the car owner and the mechanic, collections of individuals like shareholders who appoint a manager to run a company, and voters who elect a president to run a country, or they might member states of the United Nations who task that organization to coordinate responses to pandemics, implement a peacekeeping operation, and address pollution, climate change, or some other policy task that crosses national borders. The theory encompasses hierarchical relationships in private and public life. It describes a principal giving an agent a task and holding the agent accountable for the delivery of the task. If the agent fails to deliver, the principal punishes the agent or terminates the contract. Shareholders, for example, punish unsatisfactory performance by cutting a manager's pay, or replacing him. The theory simplifies the outcomes of the relationship to the interests of the parties and the information they hold. It describes the tension in the relationship produced by the different parties having conflicting interests and the principal's likely lack of relevant knowledge, or *information asymmetry*.

Viewing the relationship from the perspective of the principal, interesting questions stem from the assumption that the agent is self-interested, rather than motivated by the goals of the principal. Her challenge is to shape the agent's incentives and to limit his opportunities to exploit his position. Getting and maintaining control over the agent is central to principal-agent theory and drives much of the research. The agent's pursuit of his self-interest at the expense of the principal is the *principal-agent problem*. Borrowing from the insurance industry, the agent's opportunism is conceived as *adverse selection* and *moral hazard*. Adverse selection is the challenge facing the principal before entering the relationship; moral hazard is the concern after agreeing to delegate. Both result from the principal's information disadvantage.

Before entering the relationship, the principal lacks information about the qualities of the agent. The principal runs the risk of a poor choice of agent. The agent may be untrustworthy, unsuitable, and understandably unforthcoming about these characteristics. Like the seller of an unreliable car, or a sick person seeking health insurance, a lazy, dishonest, or incompetent agent is expected to behave rationally and to prefer to hide off-putting preexisting conditions from the principal.

After making an agreement or a contract with the agent and as the agent undertakes the task, the principal then worries about how the agent will perform and his capacity for hidden action. She worries that the agent will be tempted to act in a hidden, dishonest way at her expense. An agent may shirk rather than work, or sell a secret to the enemy. The principal cannot constantly watch the agent. Even if she can, she may not have the knowledge to know whether the agent is acting in her interest or not, for example, regarding the part he is installing in her car.

We do know from the car-maker Henry Ford that the division of labor has benefits. Yet in seeking benefits from someone else's knowledge and efforts, the principal exposes herself to the opportunism of the agent. Trust in others to carry out a task is not always repaid. There are inherent agency costs in delegating, having to do with the time and effort necessary to find the agent and to agree to the specifics of the task. They also mount up as the more far-sighted, but possibly over-anxious principal, takes costly countermeasures in order to minimize opportunism by the agent. Agency losses accrue for the principal as the self-interested agent acts against the principal's interest. Much of the principal-agent literature investigates the efficacy of the responses available to a principal to manage and deter opportunism. By exercising due diligence and not selecting high-risk candidates, by writing lengthy and elaborate contracts, by providing incentives to make opportunism less attractive, by inculcating honor codes and professional ethics, by monitoring, and by punishment and dismissal, the principal strives to deter shirking and to align the agent's interests and actions with her own.

This simple theory about the give and take and to and fro between principal and agent has great reach. Regarding a passage from Exodus about sending an angel to guide the Israelites out of Egypt, one treatment of the topic observes that "even God delegates."[3] In a passage from *Paradise Lost*, one discovers that God, too, has principal-agent problems; there are worse as well as better angels and even "Rebel Angels," which the celestial principal has to contend with and to punish (at great length). From such epic struggles to ordinary daily interactions, our understanding of a vast array of issues benefits from bringing them under the simple structure of the delegation relationship, more or less as economists have described it. It alerts us to the possibility of conflicting interests. It identifies how opportunities might be seized, helps to clarify who is in charge, and suggests how to respond to control problems. While principal-agent theory's economic applications receive the most systematic attention, thinking about control and accountability and the best response to a loss of control is a widely relevant exercise. It makes us attentive to the standards, norms, and targets ("get your numbers," as the watch commander urged) expected to guide the delivery of a task, the attribution of responsibility to the relevant actors in the delivery of a task, and, when necessary, what can be done to improve matters. What is more it suggests puzzles presented by actors not acting as the theory expects.

2

The idea behind *Why Delegate?* is to explore and to develop the logic of delegation, to show its wide application in our private and public lives, and to do so in an informal and accessible way. Of the pioneering treatments of delegation,[4] few are written for a general

---

[3] Jon Bendor, Amihai Glazer, and Thomas H. Hammond, "Theories of Delegation," *Annual Review of Political Science* 4 (2001): 235.

[4] See Kathleen M. Eisenhardt, "Agency Theory: An Assessment and Review," *The Academy of Management Review* 14, no. 1 (1989): 57–74 for a review of the early literature. See also Jean-Jacques Laffont and David Martimort, *The Theory of Economic Incentives: The Principal Agent Model* (Princeton, NJ: Princeton University Press, 2002); Bengt Holmström, "Pay for

audience as well. In the process, of course, I do not want to leave behind academic colleagues.

To contribute to understanding how we negotiate hierarchical relations in our organizational and everyday lives with real-world applications in mind, I adopt the useful terms of *principal* and *agent*, but not the mathematical language of a principal-agent theorist. In the collision of the simple, elegant theory of economists and rational choice scholars with the actual policy and practice of delegation in a variety of situations, there are, I argue, further contributions to be had in working toward a broad, more descriptively useful logic of delegation. Important insights are to be found where the principal behaves in ways that are unexpected and perhaps puzzling to a rational choice eye.[5] First, I argue and show that opportunism lies on both sides of the relationship, and nowhere as notably as when it comes to the distribution of blame.[6] Here, it is the principal who acts opportunistically at the expense of the agent. Often she does so in a way not specified in the terms on which the agent entered into the relationship. While it may be difficult to predict which tasks a principal will be willing to delegate, that is not the case with blame. Carrying off the blame is one task that decision-makers almost invariably decide to pass to an agent (or, in a passage from Leviticus, to a goat). The issue of which tasks to pass to an agent and which not is

Performance and Beyond," *American Economic Review* 107, no. 7 (2017): 1753–1777. There are excellent applications to particular policy areas, e.g., John Brehm and Scott Gates, *Working, Shirking and Sabotage* (Ann Arbor: Michigan University Press 1997), and to the bureaucracy, e.g., Gary J. Miller and Andrew B. Whitford, *Above Politics: Bureaucratic Discretion and Credible Commitment* (Cambridge: Cambridge University Press, 2015). Others have applied principal-agent theory to parliamentary government, e.g., Kaare Strom, Wolfgang C. Müller, and Torbjörn Bergman, *Cabinets and Coalition Bargaining: The Democratic Life Cycle in Western Europe* (Oxford: Oxford University Press, 2008), and to international organizations, e.g., Darren Hawkins, David Lake, Daniel Nielson, and Michael J. Tierney, *Delegation and Agency in International Organizations* (Cambridge: Cambridge University Press 2006).

[5] I thank an anonymous reviewer for challenging me about the "puzzle for the rational choice eye."

[6] Neil J. Mitchell, *Agents of Atrocity: Leaders, Followers, And the Violation of Human Rights in Civil War* (New York: Palgrave MacMillan, 2004). For an exception to the conventional focus on efficiency gains see John R. Hamman, George Loewenstein and Roberto A. Weber, "Self-Interest Through Delegation: An Additional Rationale for the Principal-Agent Relationship," *American Economic Review* 100, no. 4 (2010): 1826–1846.

an interesting question in itself. It turns out to be more complicated than the dictates of efficiency.

Second, in showing how the principal behaves in ways unexpected by the theory, the book uncovers her peculiar passivity under some conditions. Even when confronted by an agent's truly dreadful performance, an unexplored puzzle is why principals in some organizational contexts choose not to punish the opportunistic agent, as the conventional account of the relationship would lead us to expect.

On blame, *Why Delegate?* describes how shifting—or when the whistle blows, shoving—this unwelcome burden onto an agent is one of a range of incentives shaping delegation relationships. In principal-agent theory, opportunism belongs to the agent. Yet with the incentive to avoid damage to one's power and position, neither side in the delegation relationship can be trusted. A modified logic of delegation recognizes that while the division and specialization of labor and the allocation of the production and delivery of goods and services to all sorts of trades and professions are surely the engine of economic growth, the boundaries of delegation are not drawn by efficiency calculations alone. We delegate unwanted tasks, complex tasks, and sensitive, high-risk tasks. The incentives to delegate extend from efficiency calculations and saving time and effort to political calculations and saving reputations and managing the blame. It follows that although we equate the division of labor with economic and social progress, not all delegation contributes to the public good. As the motive for the division of labor and the decision to delegate shifts from the economic to the political, from saving time and effort and increasing efficiency to that of preserving power and saving reputations, delegation becomes more dubious. Sometimes the apparently rogue behavior of someone we give a task to is not a case of *can't control*, as the principal-agent theorists fear, but of *won't control*. Those in charge of the large corporation look away as contractors down the supply chain ignore child labor laws. Or when a scandal is exposed, those at the top shift the blame down to the lowest plausible level in the chain of delegation, to the "fall guy."

The success of the "fall guy" strategy rests on an intuitive acceptance by the relevant audience of the tenets of principal-agent theory.

These tenets include conflicting goals, the difficulty that those in charge have in knowing what those who work for them are up to and the presence of a control problem at the heart of the delegation relationship. An understanding of the mechanics of delegation as presented here should reveal tell-tale indicators of a principal who *won't control* rather than a principal who *can't control*. It should allow us to be more discerning judges of when individuals have genuine control problems and when individuals use delegation as a blame management device to deny responsibility and evade accountability.

The principal's claim that there was a control problem may be barely credible, but it still may offer cover for those in charge when external pressure grows for accountability. It seems enough to get a Saudi prince off the hook for the murder and dismemberment of a former advisor by his hit squad of fifteen security officials, flown in from Riyadh and fully equipped to do the deed in an Istanbul consulate in 2018.

On October 2, 2018, a trap was sprung. It was set for a fifty-nine-year-old ex-employee of the Saudi royal family, Jamal Khashoggi, at the time a columnist for the *Washington Post*. In his columns, Khashoggi wrote of the Crown Prince Mohammed bin Salman's use of repression. He compared the prince to Vladimir Putin. His final column described Saudi Arabia's loss of dignity in the Yemen war. Khashoggi was invited to the consulate in Istanbul to sort out the documents he required to wed his Turkish fiancée. She waited outside. He never came out. He was tortured, killed, and disposed of. A look-alike Khashoggi did leave the consulate.

The Riyadh arrivals that morning included members of the Crown Prince's security service. The Turkish staff in the consulate had the afternoon off. As the *Guardian* journalist Martin Chulov puts it: "The loyalties of those remaining in the building could not be questioned. The assembled hit squad was drawn from the most elite units of the Saudi security forces, whose fidelity had been repeatedly tested."[7] But, once the ghastly details of Khashoggi's fate became

[7] "Jamal Khashoggi: Murder in the Consulate," *Guardian*, October 21, 2018. https://www.theguardian.com/world/2018/oct/21/death-of-dissident-jamal-khashoggi-mohammed-bin-salman?CMP=share_btn_link.

public, their loyalty was questioned by their political master and by those who benefit from economic and strategic relationships with the Crown Prince.

The Saudis' management of the blame followed the usual sequence of denial, delay, and delegation.[8] They first denied Turkish accusations: Khashoggi had left the building and after that they knew nothing. That strategy failed. Turkish intelligence had recorded what happened. After delay, and with international attention not moving on from the Turkish revelations, the Saudis shifted to delegation. Instead of leaving the building, they claimed Khashoggi had gotten into a fight in the consulate. The squad, supposedly sent to persuade the journalist to go back to Riyadh, had gone rogue and killed him. The fidelity of this squad had been repeatedly tested, the reporting states, yet the Saudi foreign minister described a "rogue operation . . . where individuals ended up exceeding the authorities and responsibilities they had." The Crown Prince claimed not to know what his security people were doing and denounced the "heinous crime."[9] Arrests followed, and eleven faced trial in Saudi Arabia for the murder. The purpose of punishing these agents is not to correct noncompliance, as punishment is normally depicted in principal-agent theory (unless one buys the Saudi, not the Turkish version). Rather, punishment is to shift responsibility onto the agent and is an integral part of the strategy when delegation is used for blame management. Delegation, the claim of a breakdown of control, and then the punishment of individuals who were said to have implemented the killing, was an effort to buffer the Crown Prince from the blame. Others who saw the economic and strategic value of the Kingdom were now not at a total loss for words. The White House, with a stated priority of protecting its ally and its economic interests, could claim some doubt about where the buck stopped. Four months after the

[8] Neil J. Mitchell, *Democracy's Blameless Leaders: From Dresden to Abu Ghraib, How Leaders Evade Accountability for Abuse Atrocity and Killing* (New York: New York University Press, 2012).

[9] "Jamal Khashoggi Murder Trial Opens in Saudi Arabia," BBC News, January 3, 2019. https://www.bbc.co.uk/news/world-middle-east-46747332?intlink_from_url= https://www.bbc.co.uk/news/topics/czjmg5rvl57t/jamal-khashoggi-death&link_location=live-reporting-story.

killing, it was reported that at the time of Khashoggi's first column for the *Post* in September 2017, the Crown Prince had a conversation with an aide that was intercepted by the US National Security Agency. The Crown Prince had said that if the journalist could not be lured back to Saudi Arabia, he would use a bullet on him.[10] Publicly, they stuck to the "rogue operation and those responsible will be punished" story. Delegation is used, more or less successfully, for political and face-saving advantages in addition to gains in efficiency, and in ways the agent may not have bargained for.

Beyond blame and principals disingenuously claiming a lack of control, I argue that principals under some conditions can be peculiarly unresponsive. This part of the argument looks at agents organized in professions. This discussion of professionalism differs from the usual treatment in examining its costs as well as its benefits. Among agents, professionals are perhaps the one group to escape principal-agent theory with their characters tolerably unscathed. From Nobel economist Kenneth Arrow's work in the 1960s onward, a sense of professional responsibility or "idealism" is recognized as an alternative mechanism to financial incentives and to correct for opportunism. This sense of responsibility allows the principal to overcome the trust gap and the principal-agent problem. Codes of ethics and a sense of mission increase effort beyond the monetary incentive on offer, and they reduce opportunism. Yet when opportunism does occur among these agents, it repays analysis. It turns out that principals have particular difficulty addressing the rogue behavior of these agents. The paradox of professionalism is that in the process of developing the highly specialized skills that agents need for the successful accomplishment of the task, professionalism may raise singularly tenacious control issues. In some real-world contexts, the use of multiple agents, as opposed to the single agent found in the usual principal-agent models, may raise the cost of punishment and encourage passivity on the part of the principal. Where

---

[10] "Year before Killing, Saudi Prince Told Aide He Would Use 'a Bullet' on Jamal Khashoggi," *New York Times*, February 7, 2019. https://www.nytimes.com/2019/02/07/us/politics/khashoggi-mohammed-bin-salman.html.

the principal-agent theorist expects a response to correct agent opportunism, an informed but passive principal is happy to leave the hidden action hidden.

3

In short, I argue that there are modifications to be made to the standard account of the principal-agent relationship to better fit what happens in the world around us. The use of ordinary language sets the argument apart from its insurance industry origins and the formal, rational choice and game-theoretic workhorses of the economists and political scientists that give us principal-agent theory. These scholars may not see this logic of delegation as belonging in their stable, but the aim is to build on the achievements of their approach. The argument draws on the central features of principal-agent theory in seeing the interaction between those who give the orders and those who carry them out as driven by the preferences of actors, who are engaged in a struggle for information and control, anxious about betrayal, and with a capacity for opportunism. It departs from standard principal-agent theory in claiming that we should be alert to opportunism on both sides of the relationship, that the preferences of principals and agents may be substantively very different but not necessarily in conflict, that there are situations of *won't control* as well as the canonical *can't control*, and that agents may have a less rational, cooperative side, not just a competitive regard for each other. As one scales up from the individual in a relationship with a mechanic all the way to relationships between organizations on the international stage, this dynamic plays out. It is my view that an understanding of the logic of delegation can help to make sense of a marvelously disparate set of questions:

- How do we outsource tasks in our ordinary lives for ourselves or our family members?
- How do shareholders keep managers on task? Or how do those running car firms like Volkswagen ride out pollution scandals?

- What happens with more than one actor in charge? What particular difficulties do members of a "collective principal," like shareholders or owners of National Football League (NFL) teams, encounter? The team owners' agent, Commissioner Roger Goodell, hands out punishments to players and owners and attracts harsh criticism in the media. Why do not the owners rein him in?

- Was the corruption surrounding the World Cup the responsibility of the high-handed and brazen Sepp Blatter, the FIFA president? If so, why did the national football associations repeatedly re-elect him to conduct FIFA business?

- Why is an organization with such a firm view of what is right and wrong as the Catholic Church apparently indifferent to moral hazard? Like an army that ignores the war crimes of its soldiers, the church has covered up for those who use their positions in the church for private gratification. These opportunists are protected by those in charge from the negative consequences of their actions. The Catholic child abuse scandal is the biggest scandal of all time, according to the March 2019 *Atlantic Monthly* poll of *Twitter* followers (followed by the "WMD hunt" in Iraq as a distant second, then Iran-Contra and the 1919 World Series in fourth place). Does the logic of delegation help make sense of it?

- How does delegation allow principals to get away with wrongdoing? Why do states continue to delegate violence to vigilantes, motorcycle gangs, and irregular armed groups, as Russia does in Ukraine? They have regular armed forces at their disposal.

- Alternatively, how does delegation allow principals to do, or to appear to do, moral or worthy things in the face of the temptation to do otherwise? To elevate the discussion to the international level, why do member states of the United Nations delegate authority to a human rights regime, tying the hands of their own security forces?

An understanding of delegation simplifies a myriad of important and seemingly separate problems in private and public life. Attention to delegation theory helps dispel myths about, for example, the military doctrine of command responsibility and democratic accountability for abuses of human rights and provides insights on a wide variety of issues, be it corruption in FIFA or the church's child abuse scandal.

4

The approach in this book is to use diverse examples to show the variety of incentives at work and the general application of a wider logic of application. Such a strategy might be described as "cherry-picking."[11] It is certainly not random. It is also true that some cases are invitingly ripe for analysis. And there always might be other unpicked cases, out of view and awkward for the argument. The important task is not to forego illustration but to describe the argument clearly and draw out its implications in a way that opens it to empirical challenge and to further empirical research that would add confidence to the claims.

My selection of examples is driven by three concerns. First, I want to show that the theory has application to a wide range of social and political, as well as economic, real-world issues, from day care, to corporate corruption, to the Catholic Church. Much of the work in principal-agent theory is abstract. Rational choice scholars point out: "too little attention is paid to a central empirical issue: What real-world institution or process is being modeled by a particular formulation? . . . many modelers (present company included!) have been rather casual about the prima facie plausibility of their models."[12] I want to establish the prima facie plausibility of my arguments. Second, I want to show real-world applications that are of current

---

[11] I thank the anonymous reviewers for alerting me to this potential criticism. It might be applied to any who use examples to illustrate arguments, from Machiavelli to the "analytical narratives" offered by rational choice scholars within political science. With this sort of approach, theory development is on offer, but in a way that provides empirical plausibility and suggests observable implications.

[12] Bendor et al. (2001): 266–267.

concern and so I pick from the headlines. Third, I select examples that illustrate the theoretical processes at work, that are diagnostic, and that reveal puzzles unanticipated in the models. With regard to war crimes in the military, for example, I choose *the least likely case* for agents not to be held accountable by principals: the civilian-controlled armies of long-term, rule of law, Western democracies. While I cannot examine all democratic armies engaged in conflict in searching for cases awkward for the argument, I point out what sort of evidence would disconfirm my argument. In these ways, the selection of real-world examples helps develop our understanding of the logic of delegation and illustrate its usefully wide application.

5

The principal's incentives to delegate inform the structure of this work. While there is no definitive list of incentives, and others develop further subcategories, the effort is to contribute to a broader logic of delegation by examining incentives to delegate beyond efficiency gains. These incentives match different types of tasks, as illustrated in Table 1.1.

The most familiar incentives to delegate are to save time and effort and to obtain expertise. We outsource menial and disliked tasks in order to take the opportunity to spend our time more pleasantly or

Table 1.1 The Principal's Incentives and the Agent's Tasks

The Agent's Tasks	The Principal's Incentives				
	Time	Expertise	Agreement	Commitment	Blame
Menial Tasks	Chapter 2				
Complex Tasks		Chapter 3			
Judicial Tasks			Chapter 4		
Affirming Tasks				Chapter 5	
Controversial Tasks					Chapter 6

lucratively. Chapter 2 examines the incentive to save time and effort in individual and organizational contexts. For parents, it might involve finding others to look after the baby, or with surrogacy, even to make the baby. For shareholders, it involves finding managers to take proper care of their investment. For citizens, it involves electing representatives to run the government.

Some tasks are complex. We seek an agent with expertise to take out a tooth or a tumor. The challenges of delegating to professionals with specific and difficult-to-replace knowledge and training are analyzed in Chapter 3. The chapter moves from the use individuals make of professionals of one sort or another, to the use religious institutions and governments make of those with specialized training. It shows the advantages these agents extract from their positions, illustrated by control problems in the Catholic Church and in the army. Within the principal-agent literature, professionals are in good standing. Yet when these agents go bad, they may be very difficult to control. This chapter modifies the existing account with the theoretical argument that group loyalties, asset specificity, and what I refer to as the *agent confidence factor* protect these noncompliant agents from the normal consequences of their actions.

We delegate in order to resolve important disagreements. In a "friendly" tennis match, we live with the bias of our opponent, but when trophies are involved, we give the task of making the call to an umpire. When marriages get into difficulties, the couple task a therapist to get them back together, or they appeal to a judge to part. Whether disciplining players in the NFL or settling disputes between governments in the World Trade Organization, we turn to an agent to sort it out. Chapter 4 discusses the use of delegation to solve disagreements. Some depart from principal-agent theory to replace the concept of agent with that of trustee to describe the autonomy in this type of delegation relationship.[13] We can manage without this complication.

---

[13] See, for example, Karen Alter, "Delegation to International Courts and the Limits of Re-contracting Political Power," in *Delegation and Agency in International Organizations*, edited by Darren A. Hawkins, David A. Lake, Daniel L. Nielson, and Michael J. Tierney (Cambridge, UK: Cambridge University Press, 2006), pp. 312–338.

Rather than the biases of others, as Chapter 5 discusses, at times it is our own biases that we do not trust and that persuade us to delegate. There are circumstances where the principal doubts her self-control. She wishes to protect her long-term interests from ephemeral whim and desire. Or she may not lack willpower, but she expects others may doubt her determination to exercise appropriate self-control. With such doubts about, she turns to someone else, a respected agent, to affirm her trustworthiness to a valued audience. In this chapter, the incentive to delegate is to deliver on a commitment. The task for the agent is to affirm the principal's trustworthiness, despite other priorities and temptations. For a healthier future, and to keep us from short-term indulgence, we give a coach or a trainer authority over our diet and exercise regime. Or a football player finds an agent to look after the money he makes for the protracted period when no longer playing. The Argentina and Barcelona soccer star Lionel Messi used his father for this task. The pair ended up on tax fraud charges in a Spanish court. Or governments hand over the control of interest rates to central bankers in order to commit to a sound economic policy for the long term. They protect themselves from the temptation of a monetary stimulus for short-term electoral gains. More surprising at the international level, governments commit to human rights treaties and agencies, ostensibly giving up repression when dealing with opponents, dissenters, and critical journalists. While third-party or "fire-alarm" monitoring of these commitments by civil society organizations such as Amnesty International provides some added robustness to this commitment device, as the real-world application to human rights makes clear, fire alarms can be tampered with in a way unanticipated in principal-agent models.

Finally, there is the desire to evade blame for a controversial action. In Chapter 6, passing the buck is the incentive to delegate. The eighteenth-century Scottish economist Adam Smith did not underestimate the "horror of blameworthiness," which allows "neither quiet nor repose . . . from which no assurance of secrecy can protect them, from which no principle of irreligion can entirely deliver them, and from which nothing can free them but the vilest and most abject of all states, a complete insensibility to honor and infamy."[14] To avoid this horror, we delegate to a "fall guy" lower down in the organization. This task may well be hidden from the agent and not spelled out in the contract. Principals may have multiple tasks for an agent and various incentives to delegate, and these may change in the course of the delegation relationship. Blame is a task that the principal opportunistically allocates the agent when the unanticipated contingency of a whistle-blower appears on the scene and wrongdoing becomes visible. Volkswagen software engineers, hired to write code, were tasked with the blame when the scandal over diesel emissions erupted.

The question *Why Delegate?* provides an easy way into a relationship of great practical and theoretical consequence. There is more to delegation than meets the eye. We cannot take for granted that we know who is doing what for whom.

---

[14] Adam Smith, *The Theory of Moral Sentiments* (New York: Prometheus Books, [1759] 2000), p. 173.

2
Time and Effort

Taking a taxi saves the effort of driving yourself. Yet an alarming headline about cabbies' criminality adds trepidation to the journey. Wayward drivers have a private interest in mind, and not your destination. The idea that both passenger and driver, principal and agent, bring their own interests to the relationship is central to the logic of delegation. In 2015, prosecutors in London charged 413 taxi, minicab, and rickshaw drivers with criminal offenses, with 126 on the docket for violent or sexual offenses.[1] Worries created by the newspaper headline aside, the chance of getting a truly bad driver was small, with approximately 85,000 licensed vehicles in London in 2015. The odds of a safe ride were in your favor. After all, getting others to do things for us is often successful. It saves us the time and effort of doing it ourselves. Most taxi rides are uneventful.

We delegate to save time and effort. As we shift unenjoyable tasks to someone else, it may even make us happier. Some recent evidence suggests that spending money on "outsourcing menial tasks" does more for our happiness than spending on other things. Social scientists from the United States, Canada, and the Netherlands analyzed survey and field research data and found that purchasing time, as opposed to things, is an important contributor to life satisfaction. For an individual, they explain, time is finite. As a consequence, we dread "time famine," and experience "time stress." Time stress is linked to insomia, obesity, and other consequences of being too busy to exercise or eat properly. The researchers had found "a previously unexamined route from wealth to well-being: spending

---

[1] "More than 400 London Cab Drivers Charged with Crimes Last Year," *Evening Standard*, April 17, 2016. https://www.standard.co.uk/news/crime/over-400-london-cab-drivers-charged-with-crimes-last-year-a3226396.html.

Why Delegate?. Neil J. Mitchell, Oxford University Press (2021). © Oxford University Press.
DOI: 10.1093/oso/9780190904197.003.0002

money to buy free time."[2] The media, from the *Los Angeles Times* to the *BBC*, were quick to pick up on the significance of the discovery of an unexamined route to happiness. If you want to be happy, get someone else to do the shopping, mow the lawn, or clean the house. Spending money on delegating menial tasks beats a board game, a new handbag, or a bottle of wine.

One suspects that the results of the happiness study are task dependent. Simple, low-cost tasks with visible and easily measurable and attributable outcomes—you can see how the grass was cut—can be delegated successfully. The symmetrical implication would be that the harder the task is to measure and to attribute, then the more difficult it is to delegate, unless there are codes of ethics and idealism regulating the agent's effort.

While the researchers do not dwell on the downside of delegation, one surprise from this delegation-makes-you-happy study was that many people who could afford to delegate did not choose to spend money in this way. The surveys included some 800 Dutch millionaires. Almost half of this group spent no money delegating tasks they disliked. While the study did not investigate the reluctance to delegate, it did report some evidence that the relationship between time-saving purchases and happiness was not linear. At higher levels of spending, the positive benefits disappear. Higher levels of spending will amplify the inevitable trust issues that accompany an act of delegation. Before we embark on the unexamined route to happiness, we need to examine the agent.

Some university students learn this lesson the hard way. They dislike the task of writing a term paper. They pay someone else to do it for them. It is a time-saving measure. As a veteran of plagiarism tribunals at University College London, in my experience students will confess to a bad choice made to relieve time stress as multiple paper deadlines approach. Newspaper reports suggest that these particular outsourcing transactions are commonplace. As an alternative

---

[2] Ashley V. Whillans, Elizabeth W. Dunn, Paul Smeets, Rene Bekkers, and Michael I. Norton, "Buying Time Promotes Happiness," *Proceedings of the National Academy of Sciences* 144, no. 32 (2017): 8523.

to copying someone else's work, it is not without risk. I heard that one paper-writing company contacted the student's university, naming the student to whom they had supplied a "practice" paper.

Before deciding to save time in this way, a student would want to be confident about the values, as well as the competence, of the ghost writer. The student would prefer a contract with a writer who values discretion, is not too troubled by fairness concerns and is happy to remain a ghost. Deciding to cheat, the student would want to agree at the outset that the agent does a good job, but not such a good job as to arouse suspicion. He is concerned that the outsourced work might provoke disbelief beside his inarticulate and ill-informed contributions to class discussion.

Even for quite simple tasks, contracts are difficult to draft. It is hard to anticipate all contingencies that influence an outcome. Reaching an agreement is a cost incurred prior to the cost involved in monitoring the agent and checking on the timely delivery of the paper. In fact, choosing not to delegate this task and writing the paper might be easier and, who knows, might make the student happier.

This book is not a delegation-makes-you-miserable study. All the same, while outsourcing disliked tasks may be the route to happiness, it has at times been the royal road to fraud and abuse. Wherever it leads, delegation is an inescapable part of ordinary life, from at least the cradle to after the grave (we take it on trust that final wishes will be carried out). With aging, "sans teeth, sans eyes, sans taste, sans everything," our own efforts to look after ourselves are less effective. We rely on professional caregivers and financial advisers. We visit the doctor more often. We put trust in others because we can no longer do the tasks ourselves.

1

Parents want a night out. They look for a babysitter. They ask a friend and get some references to improve the odds of finding a good one. Not entirely confident of their selection, they provide the babysitter with detailed instructions. Perhaps they install a nanny cam. The cost of delegating rises. In addition to how they instruct and monitor their agent, they need to think about incentives. Setting payment at a little more than the market rate might make the agent value the task and want to come back. Getting someone who lives in the neighborhood, and whose parents live in the neighborhood, and with whom future interactions are expected, may instill a measure of accountability and might help safeguard the baby from the sitter shirking his duties and inviting his girlfriend over for the evening. The standard model of delegation points to the information disadvantages experienced by the principal and the sequence of measures the principal uses to keep control. Prior screening of agents, contracting, compensation, monitoring, and the expectation of accountability and some punishment, or the threat of the non-renewal of the contract, may keep the agent on the task.

Babysitting is not the only task that parents delegate. Some are even happy to forgo landmark achievements in the parental experience. For example, toilet-training may be outsourced to specialist contractors, such as *NYC Potty Training*. Balancing efficiency and other gains, it is possible that there may be hidden costs in delegating this task, only revealed long after the event. Looking back, might the retrospective satisfaction in parental pride be tinctured with imposter syndrome?

The accomplishment of some tasks brings intrinsic rewards and helps shape how we see ourselves. Taking professional pride in what we do is seen as a powerful motivating force in the research literature. Esprit de corps among agents substitutes for more direct incentives and replaces the need for monitoring. But this normative engagement with a task is also part of the answer to the nuanced question of how we choose to delegate specific tasks and where the boundaries of delegation may lie. Motivated by a certain idea of what it is to be a student or what it is to be a parent, there are, presumably, identity-defining tasks some want to keep to themselves.

Before the sitter arrives on the scene, "commissioning" parents may employ a surrogate to gestate and deliver a baby. By 2013 in the United States, there were over 18,000 babies born to surrogates, with a higher proportion of multiple births, as implanting two or more embryos improves the chances of success.[3] Apart from the financial barriers, there are legal, cultural, and bigotry boundaries to delegation that limit the availability of this path to parenthood. Paying someone for the months of time and effort involved in gestational services is against the law in New York. It is against the law in France and many European countries, and it has been incrementally restricted in India.

Clinics in India offered low prices to commissioning parents. But there was concern about how the arrangement was sold to surrogate mothers in the context of poverty and educational deprivation: "Madam told me I should become a surrogate and if I do, all my worries will go away . . . think of the pregnancy as 'someone's child comes to stay at your place for nine months.' "[4] In 2012, India banned same-sex couples from using surrogacy clinics. By 2016, the ban included foreigners. Business is shifting to Cambodia, Ukraine, Georgia, and elsewhere, although in Ukraine and Georgia it is only available for heterosexual couples.

There are risks on both sides of the relationship. Beyond the concern about whether the relationship between commissioning parents survives to the delivery, the surrogate mother may have to manage emotional and physical risks, which are heightened by multiple births. On their part, the principals, or commissioning parents, want a healthy baby. They purchase the surrogate's time and effort, without knowing her habits during pregnancy, or her maternal sensibilities afterward. A cross-border surrogacy adds citizenship complications with a baby born abroad.

Consequently, paid surrogacy induces lengthy contracts. One way to mitigate the uncertainty in the principal-agent relationship is to anticipate possible issues and difficulties and agree to resolutions beforehand. Even so, contingencies are hard to foresee, and the parties

---

[3] Kieran M. Perkins, Sheree L. Boulet, Denise J. Jamieson, and Dmitriy M. Kissin, "Trends and Outcomes of Gestational Surrogacy in the United States," *Fertility and Sterility* 106, no. 2 (2016): 435–442.

[4] Usha Rengachary Smerdon, "Crossing Bodies, Crossing Borders: International Surrogacy between the United States and India," *Cumberland Law Review* 39, no. 1 (2008): 50.

may not comply.[5] A surrogate gave birth to triplets in California. The seventy-five-page contract allowed for the "selective reduction" of fetuses with a multiple pregnancy. The single commissioning parent, a fifty-year-old postal worker, claimed he could not afford triplets, but the surrogate refused to abort.[6] On entering the relationship, he was unaware of the private preferences of the agent; maybe she was too.

Time moves on. We may want to live forever, but as Jonathan Swift said, we do not want to grow old—maybe with good reason where delegation is concerned. As we age, we become more dependent on delegation and, at the same time, we become less able to delegate successfully. Our ability to select and supervise an agent will decline. Our informational disadvantages are acute because of our more limited physical and mental capacity. We are less able to manage our money, as well as ourselves. Financial abuse of the elderly is described as a "virtual epidemic," and those with dementia are at especially high risk of exploitation.[7] Our agents, whether financial advisors or family members, can be opportunistic.

For those still in possession of some savings, there awaits a "five star" nursing home. To address information asymmetry, the United States government has a star rating system for nursing homes. For these facilities, the ratings have three components that reflect health standards, quality of care, and staffing. The rating system is a way to screen nursing homes and get some indication of how well the task of caring will be performed.

Seemingly simple to interpret, a weakness with the star ratings is that they depend on the nursing homes to self-report much of the data. Depending on agents to self-report is a cheap and probably biased method of auditing performance. We do not need the delegation literature to tell us that. The agent's private interest is likely to

---

[5] See Oliver Hart, "Incomplete Contracts and Control," *American Economic Review* 107, no. 7 (2017): 1731–1752.

[6] "Is a Surrogate a Mother?," *Slate*, February 15, 2016. http://www.slate.com/articles/double_x/doublex/2016/02/custody_case_over_triplets_in_california_raises_questions_about_surrogacy.html?via=gdpr-consent.

[7] Mark S. Lachs and Karl A. Pillemer, "Elder Abuse," *New England Journal of Medicine* 373 (2015): 1947–1956.

warp the reporting to the agent's advantage. Of the three components of the rating, only health inspections are conducted externally and so are less susceptible to manipulation. The system's critics point out that the care homes provide misleading information and furthermore that the ratings leave out highly relevant material such as consumer complaints and fines.[8] The choice of whom to trust with the care of our nearest and dearest is difficult.

It is not a decision to get wrong. In some nursing homes, there is violence perpetrated either by other residents or by the staff.[9] It is hard to believe, but an eighty-three-year-old woman, who as a girl fled Indonesia in fear of rape by Japanese soldiers, seventy years later was raped in a Minnesota care center. By then she had Alzheimer's disease. On December 18, 2014, at 4:30 in the morning, a nursing assistant attacked her. She was unable to defend herself, unable to raise the alarm, and unable to report what was done to her. The nursing assistant had been suspended three times as a consequence of prior allegations of sexual assaults. On this occasion, he was caught in the act by another staff member. A shocking CNN investigation, "Sick, Dying and Raped in America's Nursing Homes," details this and other appalling cases of abuse and humiliation.[10] As the report suggests, the often chaotic conditions of these homes is an environment that encourages predation. With patients harassing and abusing other patients, the lightly staffed and supervised night shift allows those providing the care to shirk in one way or another. The poor pay may make it difficult to recruit those with the right disposition for the task. Those charged with providing care are in a powerful position, as those they care for often have difficulty providing a coherent account of what happens to them. The CNN report cites US federal government data on 16,000 sexual abuse complaints between 2000 and 2015 with over 1,000 nursing homes not responding

[8] "Medicare Star Ratings Allow Nursing Homes to Game the System," *New York Times*, August 24, 2014. https://www.nytimes.com/2014/08/25/business/medicare-star-ratings-allow-nursing-homes-to-game-the-system.html.

[9] Lachs and Pillemer (2015), p. 1947.

[10] CNN, February 22, 2017. https://edition.cnn.com/interactive/2017/02/health/nursing-home-sex-abuse-investigation/.

appropriately to allegations of sexual abuse. The number of actual cases may be substantially higher, given the vulnerability of the victims, their difficulties reporting, and perhaps a general disbelief that anyone would want to do these things to the very old and infirm.

A tragic irony is that those with the least amount of time left are likely to have the most difficulty purchasing time successfully. Their information disadvantage is extreme. In addition to physical, sexual, and financial abuse, the old risk psychological and verbal mistreatment, not to mention simple neglect, whether in terms of nutrition, hydration, medication, or hygiene. The lawyers and police consulted in the CNN (2017) report on sexual abuse called for improved training for caregivers, and better supervision and monitoring. The prior issue is selection and knowing the private interests and competence of the agents, and then knowing what they are doing when they take care of our aged relatives. In turn, the size of the pool of agents who offer to perform these tasks depends on the financial incentives to work in a nursing home. A bundle of responses is likely to be most effective. As we scale up from these individual interactions to business and to other organizations and settings, we see the same struggle for information and control.

2

In Tolstoy's novel *Anna Karenina*, the well-meaning Russian estate owner, Constantin Levin, wondered why he delegated agricultural tasks. His frustrations with life on the farm are thought to correspond with Tolstoy's experience in running his estate. Levin describes the goal conflict with his agricultural laborers:

> But now he clearly saw . . . that the agricultural work he was carrying on was founded on a bitter and obstinate struggle between himself and his labourers. . . . What was the essential cause of that hostility? He struggled to get every penny he could, and had to do so or he would not have been able to pay his labourers their wages, and they struggled to be allowed to work quietly, pleasantly, and just as they were used to work.

It was to his interest that every labourer should get through as much work as possible and at the same time give his mind to it, not injuring the winnowing machine, the horse-rake, or the threshing machine, but working intelligently. The labourer wished to work in the pleasantest way possible, with intervals of rest . . . the labourers wished to work merrily and without care, while his interests were not only foreign and incomprehensible to them but flatly opposed to their own just interests.[11]

Levin worried about sabotage and shirking by those working for him. The flat opposition of interests underlying the principal-agent problem (leaving aside love's distractions) was the root cause of his lost enthusiasm for farming.

While this problem shapes modern economic relationships, in contrast to Levin, the multiple individual owners of firms generally do not have the time to oversee the running of the business. They add a link to the chain of delegation and entrust a manager to do it for them. And prudent investors diversify their portfolios, providing little incentive for them to give detailed attention to the management of any single firm.[12] In turn, managers delegate tasks to their workforce or they outsource to other firms, for example, to a textile factory in a country with lax labor laws. The decision to delegate may be motivated by the expectation of efficiency gains that make it worthwhile to pay someone else to put in the time and effort for the task. But principals also fear that agents will seek to "work merrily and without care" and they, in turn, will seek a response to such opportunism. There is a large research literature to help our understanding of the chains of delegation linking shareholders and managers, employers and employees, and global corporations and offshore suppliers. There are powerful incentives to delegate, yet as the literature tells us, it persists only because of the devices developed to allay worries about shirking, sabotage, and other forms of agent opportunism.

[11] Leo Tolstoy, *Anna Karenina* (New York. Dover Publications, [1877] 2012), pp. 289–290.
[12] Eugene Fama, "Agency Problems and the Theory of the Firm," *The Journal of Political Economy* 88, no. 2 (1980): 288–307.

It usually takes a substantial shock to create sufficient disquiet with the status quo to galvanize shareholders to take control of their agents. Reckitt Benckiser's $17 billion takeover of baby-food manufacturer Mead Johnson triggered enormous bonus payments to managers. Shareholders found these payments hard to swallow. The company compensation committee responded to the shareholder protests and the chief executive Rakesh Kapoor took a pay cut.[13] He has since retired. These assertions of control are rare enough to make the headlines. Agency loss has to be flagrant for shareholders to become motivated and for the CEO to go.

3

In part, shareholders are disadvantaged because there are so many of them. They have to come together to form a collective, rather than single, principal. Members of collective principals have two handicaps, stemming from the preferences they do and do not share. First, in contrast to a single principal, they will likely have differences in preferences from issue to issue. These different preferences may provide a clever agent with the opportunity to cultivate and even create factions within the collective principal in order to increase discretion, as a guileful child plays off parents against each other to get what she wants.

The National Football League Commissioner Roger Goodell serves as the agent of a collective principal, the thirty-two owners of teams in the National Football League. Among his quite varied tasks, he negotiates deals with television companies and the players' representatives on behalf of the owners. NFL revenues have increased dramatically coincident with Goodell becoming commissioner in 2006. The NFL owners may know the financial outcome for the NFL, but not what effort or luck produced this result. A feature of the principal-agent relationship is that normally the principal cannot

---

[13] "Reckitt Cuts Pay of Chief Executive," *Financial Times*, March 28, 2018. https://www.ft.com/content/851f3502-328a-11e8-ac48-10c6fdc22f03.

observe the agent's effort and isolate an agent's contribution, which complicates evaluation and incentives. All the same, the financial success of an enterprise disposes profit-oriented owners to stick with a manager, or for that matter a commissioner.

Whether another choice of agent would have been as beneficial for them is not known, but the owners have repeatedly renewed Goodell's contract. Goodell does not take his renewal for granted. At his place of work, he is known to intone, "only the paranoid survive," the title of a book by Andrew Grove, the CEO of Intel.[14] Beyond mantras and profitability, Goodell's survival is assisted by the institutional structure of the delegation relationship. Some members of the collective principal are more influential than others. According to those who know the NFL, "Goodell is an expert at managing up, and he has learned that the key to succeeding—and more recently, surviving . . . is by identifying and leaning on 'four or five owners that Roger uses to run the league.'"[15] Until recently, Dallas Cowboys owner Jerry Jones has been one of the influential group of owners Goodell leans on. The Dallas Cowboys were valued at $4.8 billion in 2017, which made them the most valuable team in the league, and of any sports franchise worldwide. The average worth of an NFL team was $2.5 billion.[16] While all the teams benefit from the commissioner's negotiation of lucrative television deals and good collective bargaining terms with the players, some teams have more at stake than others. As we shall see in a later chapter, in addition to making deals for the owners, he is tasked with enforcing the rules of the game and resolving disputes. Goodell's exercise of discretion in the handling of this task is necessarily visible and highly

[14] "Roger Goodell's Unstoppable Football Machine," *New York Times*, February 3, 2016. https://www.nytimes.com/2016/02/07/magazine/roger-goodells-unstoppable-football-machine.html.

[15] Kent Babb, "How Roger Goodell Became the Most Powerful Man in American Sports," *Washington Post*, September 3, 2015. https://www.washingtonpost.com/gdpr-consent/?next_url=https%3a%2f%2fwww.washingtonpost.com%2fsports%2fredskins%2fhow-roger-goodell-became-the-most-powerful-man-in-american-sports%2f2015%2f09%2f02%2f3eb69baa-50d8-11e5-9812-92d5948a40f8_story.html.

[16] "The Dallas Cowboys Head the NFL's Most Valuable Teams at $4.8 Billion," *Forbes* September 18, 2017. https://www.forbes.com/sites/kurtbadenhausen/2017/09/18/the-dallas-cowboys-head-the-nfls-most-valuable-teams-at-4-8-billion/?sh=25f16ed0243f.

controversial. Jones had bitter words for Goodell over the punishment of a Cowboy running-back. Goodell may have to cultivate some of the other owners as he serves out his latest renewal as commissioner. The varied preferences likely to be found among members of a collective principal make it more difficult to assert control over the agent.

The second handicap of the collective principal, as with any group, is one preference that they will all have in common: the temptation for members of a group to shirk group tasks and to free-ride on the work of others. As the size of the group increases, from say the thirty-two owners of the NFL to shareholders in a large corporation, this handicap becomes more severe. In addition to the usual information advantages an agent enjoys, one who is accountable to a collective principal, and who wants to do as he likes, has the "logic of collective action" on his side.[17] The varied preferences and different stakes of the multiple actors are likely to make a collective principal's oversight effort less consistent. Members of the collective principal have the temptation to free-ride on the task of managing the agent. All members of the collective principal benefit from a well-supervised agent performing up to expectations, whether or not an individual member contributed much to oversight. Absent a crisis, the likely strategy is to leave the task of monitoring and voicing concerns to someone else. In the corporation, managers may take advantage of inactive shareholders to improve the view from their office, add to their financial well-being, build an empire, and otherwise benefit themselves at the owners' expense.

In the light of all that might happen, the puzzle is why shareholders part with their money. Why delegate? In raising this question, economists Andrei Shleifer and Robert Vishny examine the reputation of managers, investor optimism, and the internal and external mechanisms available to protect the shareholder in the running of the corporation.[18] As they point out, the mechanisms to keep

---

[17] Mancur Olson, in the *Logic of Collective Action* (Cambridge MA: Harvard University Press, 1965) explains the difficulty of achieving cooperation for some collective purpose among self-interested parties.

[18] Andrei Shleifer and Robert W. Vishny, "A Survey of Corporate Governance," *The Journal of Finance* 52, no. 2 (1997): 737–783; see Anup Agrawal and Tommy Cooper, "Corporate

managers in line work well enough for investment to flow, but they could be improved.

One institutional device to look after the collective principal's interests is to add another link to the chain of delegation by electing a board of directors. Boards typically have available the familiar selection, incentive, and punishment mechanisms used to align agents' performance with the principal's preferences.[19] These boards appoint or terminate managers, they determine their compensation, and they approve important decisions.

But boards have a mixed record in providing oversight of managerial decision-making. Voting in board elections requires some effort, and with a large number of investors, individual investors may not bother to participate. They may not think it worthwhile to inform themselves about the candidates and to participate in electing a high-quality group with a degree of independence from the managers that the board is supposed to oversee. Managers may chair the board to which they are accountable. They may protect their information advantage by influencing the membership and the agenda of the board. But if there is an independent shareholder on the board, one with a large stake in the firm's performance, then that shareholder has the incentive to absorb the monitoring costs and engage in proper oversight of the management rather than free-ride, and this improves performance indicators.[20]

There are external safeguards of shareholders' interests. These, too, are only likely to be triggered late in the day. The threat of takeover or bankruptcy may help align managers' interests with the owners. Imperfect control of their agents aside, money continues to flow from these shareholders. If not just for the want of a better place to put it, as the scholars of corporate governance suggest, it may be due to most managers valuing their reputations and seeking

Governance Consequences of Accounting Scandals: Evidence from Top Management CEO and Auditor Turnover," *Quarterly Journal of Finance* 7, no. 1 (2016): 1–41.

[19] See Michael C. Jensen "The Modern Industrial Revolution, Exit, and the Failure of Internal Control Systems," *The Journal of Finance* 48, no. 3 (1993): 831–880

[20] Anup Agrawal and Tareque Nasser, "Blockholders on Boards and CEO Compensation, Turnover and Firm Valuation," *Quarterly Journal of Finance* 9, no. 3 (2019): 1–67.

to improve their chances in the managerial labor market, or to the gambler within us and the irrepressible optimism of investors.

4

Maintaining investors' optimism involves, in the next link in the chain of delegation, managers overseeing a productive workforce. In the struggle for control between principal and agent, product terrain makes a difference. Managers look to seize the high ground and command an unimpeded view of what their employees are doing.

In contrast to the crude and occasional mechanisms shareholders use to assert control over managers, call centers allow supervisors minute-by-minute observation of the agent working the phones. From the start to the finish of the shift, management monitors how workers use their time. Information asymmetry is negligible. Undercover sociologist Jamie Woodcock describes the call center where he worked: "the workers . . . felt the power of the management gaze constantly. The fear of a recorded conversation coming back to haunt a worker—or worse deny them of their monthly bonus—kept behaviour in check."[21] In this workplace, monitoring what the agent is doing is easy. It is not reliant on self-reports. The call is scripted. Information on the content, duration, and success of calls is recorded. Fake phoning gets you fired. There is little scope for hidden action. Yet here, too, where so little is left to the agent's discretion, delegation involves costs as well as gains. The costs of a surveillance approach to management appear to be substantial. Too visible a lack of trust and too much effort to prevent shirking takes its toll on a workforce. Stress and consequently labor turnover in call centers are high.

The call center, through its monitoring procedures, reduces the problem of hidden action, at least among the callers. But supervisors evaluate the information received on callers' performance. In

---

[21] Jamie Woodcock, *Working the Phones Control and Resistance in Call Centres* (London: Pluto Press, 2017), p. 7.

the center where the sociologist worked, in order to protect their bonuses at the end of each month, the supervisors took measures to "hide" the poor performances of callers in their reports: "the bonuses affected the supervisors' behaviour; they would even devise strategies that undermined the profitability of the call centre to safeguard their bonuses . . . workers who were most likely to make bad calls were kept off the phones."[22]

Working in a call center is an intense experience. Those at the other end of the phone line may want an emotional connection. It is not simply the words that are said on the phone that matter. The tone is important. One study reports stress levels for a call center worker as exceeding those of a coal miner, with 80 percent of the workers surveyed wanting help in managing stress.[23] But agents are easily replaceable, and turnover is an accepted cost. Jamie Woodcock reports that he was one of the longest serving of his entering group. His incentive was to gather material for his book on call centers.

Aside from giving us a more sympathetic ear for the human being at the other end of the phone line, attention to call center operations illustrates the costs ever present in delegation, even where the direct cost of auditing is low.

5

"Do you want to know my real age or my factory age?" asked a young girl working in a clothing factory in Myanmar that supplies various multinationals.[24] The girl's poignant question reflects the competing pressures influencing decisions in a global corporation. Firms outsource production to agents around the world for efficiency gains.

---

[22] Ibid., p. 70.

[23] See Catriona M. Wallace and Geoff Eagleson, "The Sacrificial HR Strategy in Call Centers," *International Journal of Service Industry Management* 11 no. 2 (2000): 178; Gavin Poynter, "Emotions in the Labour Process," *European Journal of Psychotherapy, Counselling, & Health* 5, no. 3 (2002): 247–261.

[24] "How High Street Clothes Were Made by Children In Myanmar for 13p an Hour," *The Observer*, February 5, 2017. https://www.theguardian.com/world/2017/feb/05/child-labour-myanmar-high-street-brands.

Yet the corporation would prefer not to be seen to be taking advantage of children, even if local laws permit child labor, as they do in Myanmar.

This preference may come from within the corporation or, more likely, from without. It is possible that corporate managers simply do the right thing. It is more likely that they assume any extra "social responsibility" costs of delegating to contractors in the developing world in response to pressure from other actors. Unions and civil society organizations, such as Human Rights Watch and Amnesty International, press for universal standards and the protection of workers' rights. The pressure operates through the reputational consequences of being exposed to be visibly doing the wrong thing in outsourcing for efficiency gains. The consequences are felt through shifts in the behavior of consumers, investors, the corporate workforce, or legislators. Such pressure has a long and sometimes successful history. The eighteenth-century campaign to abolish the slave trade, which British shipping dominated at the time, was led by the Society for Effecting the Abolition of the Slave Trade, and included consumer boycotts of sugar and rum from the West Indies. Nike faced a student-led boycott of its products in the 1990s over its use of sweatshops.

In choosing to delegate, how can the corporate principal resolve the competing pressures, on the one hand, to be profitable (where the girl has a factory age) and, on the other hand, to be ethical (where the girl has a real age)? One option is not to delegate. A corporation may choose not to outsource. The downside is in disappointing the ultimate principal, the shareholder, and endangering its competitive position if other corporations continue to enjoy the lower costs of production that result from the time and effort of children. The corporation may choose to ignore external social pressure. But it anticipates an uncertain set of possibly negative consequences, whether from boycotts or regulation. To finesse these options, the corporation may maintain its global supply chains while advertising an ethical commitment to a code of conduct.

There is an impressive superstructure of corporate cares and commitments built on overseas trade and investment. These commitments are sector specific, such as the chemical industry's Responsible Care Initiative and the Extractive Industries Transparency Initiative, and are contained in more general frameworks, such as the Ethical Trading Initiative and the United Nations Global Compact. Launched by United Nations Secretary General Kofi Annan in 2000, the UN Global Compact claims to be the "world's largest corporate sustainability initiative."[25] Over 9,500 companies from 160 countries had joined the Global Compact by 2020, declaring adherence to universal human rights, labor rights, environmental, and anti-corruption standards.

Yet what of the integrity of this superstructure, if it rests on lower costs and if it is propped up only by external pressure? A corporation's cares and commitments are often framed in terms of its awareness of multiple "stakeholders." It is unlikely that in the day-to-day running of the corporation, all these stakeholders are equal. Despite the shareholder's imperfect control, their measurable interests are likely to prevail in a contest for a manager's attention. On the other hand, it is unlikely that external pressure from civil society, perhaps severe in a crisis, will last. The temptation is to reap the expected reputational benefits to be gained from participating in a social responsibility initiative, without a serious commitment of resources.

The spread of these commitments and corporate social responsibility initiatives suggests that corporations continue to find them a useful way out of production dilemmas. Those who created the United Nations Global Compact were aware of its deficiencies. Given the weakness of the international community in promulgating and enforcing universal standards, some system of private governance and self-regulation is all that is available in a world where the power to regulate remains with rivalrous nation-states. The designers of these initiatives worked on the basis of encouraging the diffusion of new norms of business. The motivating idea is that norm diffusion

[25] See John Gerard Ruggie, "Reconstituting the Global Public Domain: Issues, Actors, and Practices," *European Journal of International Relations* 10, no. 4 (2004): 499–531; Patrick Bernhagen and Neil Mitchell, "The Private Provision of Public Goods," *International Studies Quarterly* 54 no. 4 (2010): 1175–1187.

between civil society and global corporations will spread good practice.

One indicator of the sincerity of corporate social responsibility, beyond announcing the standards and codes of conduct, would be in the observable measures the corporate managers take to overcome information asymmetry down the chain of delegation. What do they do about monitoring the supply chain? The presence of monitoring does not mean that factories will be following the rules, but the absence of monitoring suggests a hollow commitment. There are two main approaches to monitoring, in addition to self-reporting. The principal may set up auditing machinery or can rely on external third parties, in this case international organizations such as the United Nations, civil society groups, and labor rights campaigners, to sound the *fire alarm*.[26] One problem with auditing machinery is who audits the auditors?[27] As the girl's question makes clear, even the presence of monitoring in the form of factory visits may not be reason for confidence in the integrity of the monitoring and the sincerity of commitments, adding to the importance of scrutiny by external civil society groups.

In 2013, the Rana Plaza building in Bangladesh, a building certified as compliant with international standards, collapsed.[28] It took five clothing factories down with it. Over 1,100 industry workers died. Reportedly, only by searching the ruins for brand labels was it possible to know which companies sourced their products from these factories.[29] Out of the shock and the rubble of Rana Plaza

[26] Matthew D. McCubbins and Thomas Schwartz, "Congressional Oversight Overlooked: Police Patrols versus Fire Alarms," *American Journal of Political Science* 28, no. 1 (1984): 165–179.

[27] Experiments with pollution monitoring in India suggests ways to improve monitoring effectiveness. See Esther Duflo, Michael Greenstone, Rohini Pande and Nicholas Ryan, "Truth-Telling by Third-Party Auditors and the Response of Polluting Firms: Experimental Evidence from India," Massachusetts Institute of Technology, Department of Economics Working Paper Series (July 17, 2013).

[28] Peter Lund-Thomsen and Adam Lindgreen, "Corporate Social Responsibility in Global Value Chains: Where Are We Now and Where Are We Going?," *Journal of Business Ethics* 123, no. 1 (2014): 11–22.

[29] Human Rights Watch, "Follow the Thread: The Need for Supply Chain Transparency in the Garment and Footwear Industry," April 20, 2017. https://www.hrw.org/report/2017/04/20/follow-thread/need-supply-chain-transparency-garment-and-footwear-industry.

emerged a coalition of civil society groups and unions, including Human Rights Watch, the Clean Clothes Campaign, and the International Trade Union Confederation. They sought to restructure the relationship between global multinational corporations and the local agents they selected to produce apparel. This coalition created a Transparency Pledge. The coalition contacted global apparel and footwear companies to reveal information about their supply chains and the names and addresses of the factories they were using. Some twenty-nine of the seventy-two companies contacted by Human Rights Watch to sign the Transparency Pledge had committed to release some information about the factories they used. Hugo Boss and Walmart, among others, resisted the pressure for transparency.[30]

A very few companies, such as Nike, had already identified the local agents they used. But analysts of Nike's efforts to improve working conditions among its suppliers are not optimistic about the efficacy of monitoring alone. With over 800 local factories supplying its footwear and apparel, Nike's monitoring task is very costly.[31] Despite the company's investment in an internal auditing bureaucracy, "analyses of the company's own data suggest that conditions have improved somewhat in some of its suppliers but either stagnated or deteriorated in many others. . . . In short, monitoring alone is not producing the large and sustained improvements in workplace conditions that many had hoped it would."[32] Monitoring is a necessary, not sufficient, condition for companies to deliver on their commitments.

Some research on the protection of worker rights suggests that global corporations contracting with suppliers in developing countries are associated with reduced protection consistent with a "race to the bottom" dynamic.[33] Multinationals look abroad for

---

[30] NPR, "Four Years after Rana Plaza Tragedy, What's Changed for Bangladeshi Garment Workers?" April 30, 2017. https://www.npr.org/sections/parallels/2017/04/30/525858799/4-years-after-rana-plaza-tragedy-whats-changed-for-bangladeshi-garment-workers.

[31] Lund-Thomsen and Lindgreen (2014).

[32] Richard M. Locke, Fei Qin, and Alberto Brause, "Does Monitoring Improve Labor Standards? Lessons from Nike," *Industrial and Labor Relations Review* 61, no. 1 (2007): 21.

[33] Layna Mosley and David A. Singer, "Migration, Labor, and the International Political Economy," *Annual Review of Political Science* 18 (2015): 283–301.

cheaper labor. Their agents in the developing world have to attract orders on that basis. Firms in developing countries compete on the price of labor, and with limited alternatives their governments facilitate that, perhaps in the form of lax enforcement of labor rights. At both ends of the outsourcing relationship, powerful incentives and the weakness of monitoring undermine the diffusion of labor rights around the world. Rana Plaza did spur firms to offset reputational damage and cooperate with civil society initiatives, but the protection of labor rights is one of Kofi Annan's "problems without a passport." It takes the international cooperation of governments around the world to address these types of problems more effectively.

6

Citizens, like shareholders, delegate, and for similar reasons. The running of the country, like the firm, requires time and effort. Conceiving the relationship of citizens to rulers as an act of delegation is rooted in liberal political philosophy. It is a conception that gave birth to revolutions. The American revolutionary war against the British had life, liberty, and the pursuit of happiness as its declared goals. The Declaration asserted that these were self-evident truths and unalienable rights given "man" by the Creator. Governments are tasked to secure these rights. The truths were not self-evident to King George III, and there are alternative Creators uninterested in endowing worshippers and heretics with a common set of rights. Then, more importantly, the Declaration described government as deriving its powers from the consent of the governed.

The train of thought got going in the previous century. It was another unintended philosophical legacy of resisting another oppressive monarch. Charles I was executed in central London in January 1649. The loser in the English Civil War, he was held responsible by the parliamentary side for the conflict recurring in 1648. For his part, Charles took beheading with dignity. Historians quote from Macbeth: "nothing in his life became him like the leaving of it." Now the problem for the new English Commonwealth was the king's posthumous popularity. To respond to the volatile public mood, parliament enlisted the poet John Milton (1608–1674). Milton opposed tyranny of all sorts, whether in the form of censorship of the printing presses, marriage without the option of divorce, or a monarch violating fundamental rights and freedoms. On his European travels in the 1630s, Milton met with Galileo Galilei, who was under house arrest in Florence, a grim augury for the English tourist who was also determined to tell the truth as he observed it.

Indicative of the public mood and the controversy over the monarch's fate, the identity of the executioner of Charles I is unknown. He was in disguise. In contrast, Milton very visibly revealed his support for the trial and punishment of the monarch in *The Tenure of Kings and Magistrates*. Many on the parliamentary side had absented themselves from the proceedings, and for some of those "regicides" who signed the death warrant there was fatal reckoning with the restoration of Charles II in 1660.

Milton's reasoning for the regime-changing choice made by parliament was offered to the public just two weeks after the execution (a second edition followed in 1650). He pointed out that the English people had a principal-agent problem. Milton began on a note of disappointment. Individuals tend not to think for themselves. They do not use reason. Instead, they follow custom and "blind affections." This intellectual surrender explains ongoing loyalty to their unreliable royal agent. Milton's argument is more ambitious than the immediate context, and he asserts that all "men" are born free, whether or not divided by "the English Sea." He depicts kings as agents of the people and in a contractual relationship. For "ease" or convenience, kings are provisionally entrusted with power by the people to govern. That power is revocable if it is misused: "It being thus manifest, that the power of Kings and Magistrates is nothing else, but what is only derivative, transferr'd, and committed to them in trust from the People, to the Common good of them all, in whom the power yet remains fundamentally, and cannot be tak'n from them, without a violation of thir natural birthright."[34] A free and reasoning "people" is Milton's collective principal, and they have the right to throw the royal rascal out, or worse, if he does not deliver. The principal may withdraw the grant of authority from political leaders, if they govern at the expense of the people's welfare. He wrote to address an urgent political problem, the undeserved popularity of a dead monarch, headless in Whitehall. Yet Milton's imagining of an ultimate principal as the source of political power made clear the provisional basis on which it was granted. It was a thought experiment where rational individuals hold government to account.

Subsequently, the social contract theorists Thomas Hobbes and John Locke developed versions of this approach, but differed on the "right to rebellion." Power once given to Hobbes's Leviathan was irrevocable—the price of security—while Locke was closer to Milton with the idea that the act of political delegation represented a limited and accountable grant of authority, which could be withdrawn. Milton enumerates the wrongs done by tyrants with unaccountable power: "murders, massachers, rapes, adulteries, desolation."[35] For him, the institutions and practices of a republic founded on delegation, not custom or bias, would protect against these wrongs. Deeply religious as he was, religion for Milton was an "unforcible thing." In a later work, he appealed to Oliver Cromwell, leader of the new regime, to "always take the side of those who think that not just their own party or faction, but all citizens equally have an equal right to freedom in the state."[36] After Cromwell's death and the restoration of the monarchy in 1660, Milton was briefly arrested for his writings. Long since blind, another affliction shared with Galileo, his later years were devoted to his poetry. *Paradise Lost* and other works put his political theory in the shade. But Milton's contribution to our understanding of the contractual relationship between ruler and

[34] John Milton, "The Tenure of Kings and Magistrates," in *John Milton Prose: Major Writings on Liberty, Politics, Religion, and Education,* edited by David Loewenstein (Oxford: Wiley-Blackwell, [1650] 2013), p. 250.

[35] Ibid., 254.

[36] Milton, "A Second Defence of the English People," in *John Milton Prose: Major Writings on Liberty, Politics, Religion, and Education,* edited by David Loewenstein (Oxford: Wiley-Blackwell, [1654] 2013), 373.

ruled matters. His way of reasoning about freedom as an individual "birthright" prior to government and as a restraint on the activities of governments is with us today.

To make democracy work, we elect parliaments and presidents. We do not have the time for the agora, even a virtual one, and the plethora of issues requiring our attention. We authorize our agents to rule for a period of time on our behalf. Like principals generally, we hope our trust in them is repaid. If not, we dismiss them at the next election.

As with the selection of any agents, choosing those who make political decisions on our behalf is challenging. The competition among candidates for our votes reveals some information about how they will conduct themselves and how well their policy preferences match our own. But adverse selection is likely. Even before the campaign begins, the characteristics of the market for votes and the presence of "inferior candidates" may put off good-quality candidates coming forward.[37] Money, media influence, and manipulation distort the quality of information available to the voter. Once in office, and perhaps for good as well as ill, we have limited means to control elected officials. If the incentive to delegate is time and we conceive electing representatives as a device to manage time deficits, then we expect them to reflect our preferences, as far as they know them. We limit their discretion. If the incentive to delegate is as a device to manage cognitive and knowledge deficits, then we expect them to deliberate for us and decide in the public interest. We increase their discretion.

The eighteenth-century conservative philosopher Edmund Burke conceptualized these two political agent roles as those of a delegate, on the one hand, or a trustee, on the other. A delegate mirrors his constituency. A trustee acts on its behalf, as best as her conscience and knowledge guide her.[38] A century later, John Stuart

---

[37] See George A. Akerlof, "The Market for "Lemons": Quality Uncertainty and the Market Mechanism," *The Quarterly Journal of Economics* 84, no. 3 (1970): 488–500.

[38] For a more nuanced treatment of representation, see Andrew Rehfeld, "Representation Rethought: On Trustees, Delegates, and Gyroscopes in the Study of Political Representation and Democracy," *American Political Science Review* 103, no. 2 (2009): 214–230.

Mill, in *Considerations on Representative Government*, explained why we delegate in politics. We have not improved much on his argument and not just the practical point about the size of political communities, the large number of decisions to be made, and the infeasibility of direct rule. He took human beings as they are. Their preferences are likely selfish. They suffer from what is now labeled the "time inconsistency problem," or knowing how to balance short-term against long-term well-being. Improvidently, says Mill, voters tend to prefer "present to distant interests."[39] Delegation is a means to gear decisions to more distant interests and commitments and long-term well-being, rather than the temptations of immediate gratification. But our representatives themselves have a hard time looking beyond the present election cycle and may choose re-election over the greater good.

Mill noted the selection problem and the possibility that the electoral process puts off better candidates from running for election. He argued for a particular set of electoral rules to mitigate this problem. He wanted representatives capable of fulfilling a "trustee" role and able to bring specialist knowledge to bear on policy questions. He described the parliamentary system of democracy as a chain of delegation. Voters elect the legislature, which itself does not govern, but scrutinizes a government that is responsible to it. The next link in the chain is between individual members of the government, department ministers, and the appointed officials of the bureaucracy. Individual ministers take responsibility for the performance of a meritocratic civil service. The main check in the system is making representatives answerable to the electorate periodically. The individual voter, Mill argued, is ultimately the only "safe guardian" of her own rights and interests. He supported female suffrage. In aggregate, these voters encourage decisions that contribute to the general welfare.

Mill had doubts about the US presidential system, given the likelihood of outsiders with little experience in government being

---

[39] John Stuart Mill, *Considerations on Representative Government* (Rockville, MD: Serenity, [1861] 2008), p. 81.

elected. Following Mill, political scientists contrast the performance of the different types of representative democracy. Kaare Strom and colleagues compare the type and amount of agency loss that parliamentary and presidential systems are likely to experience.[40] Given a government's control of the legislature and party discipline, there are few checks on the power of a parliamentary government between elections. The consequence is that the likelihood of agency loss and governments making policy diverging from the preferences of the collective principal is greater in parliamentary systems. A determined leader with strong policy convictions in a parliamentary system, for example British Prime Minister Margaret Thatcher, may lead rather than follow the preferences of voters in privatizing the economy, dismantling the welfare state, and dealing with terror and military threats at home and abroad. Presidential systems separate rather than fuse powers. The legislature and executive are elected in separate elections and on different election cycles. A president has more institutional checks on his discretion and less opportunity for hidden action than a prime minister in a parliamentary system with a majority in the legislature.

Politicians' terms of office normally go on until we select someone else at the next election. In assessing performance or anticipating future policy, electorates may prioritize how well politicians perform the economic task, which is significant in its impact on their lives, and it is measurable. But as is often the case with delegation, agents multitask and do some things better than others, making performance evaluation more difficult, and while an outcome may become known to voters, for example the unemployment rate or the size of the deficit, it is not easy to attribute the agent's responsibility in delivering the outcome. On the campaign trail, the agent's self-report to the principal may not be reliable. Were the good economic numbers because of the president's decisions, or in spite of them?

---

[40] See Kaare Strom, Wolfgang C. Muller, and Torbjorn Bergman, eds., *Delegation and Accountability in Parliamentary Democracies* (Oxford: Oxford University Press, 2006).

7

In office, of all the tasks a government undertakes, it is the exercise of violence that distinguishes it. Coercion is the property of the state. In fact, Thomas Hobbes, writing in the wake of the English Civil War, and later the German sociologist Max Weber defined the state as monopolizing violence. It is one task not to be outsourced. More recently, Nobel economist Douglas North and coauthors, in *Violence and Social Orders*, describe the handing of weapons over to a professional military as a pivotal moment in the formation of modern states and in social and economic development.[41] Even those who explicitly recognize the efficiencies gained from reducing the size of the public sector and privatizing supplies and services exclude violence from the prescription. Some tasks are what political scientist James Q. Wilson labels "sovereign tasks" and are not to be outsourced; these tasks require the authority that only states possess. Drawing on Wilson's work, Nobel economist Oliver Williamson used the concept of "probity hazard" to further develop the idea of sovereign tasks, to explain why violence should not be delegated, and to establish the boundary between what is to be delivered by the public and private sectors. Probity refers to the "loyalty and rectitude" of agents in carrying out a task. On the surface, this concept adds little to the theory of delegation. The fear of untrustworthy agents is fundamental to principal-agent theory. What distinguishes the probity hazard from the ordinary hazards of a principal-agent relationship is the magnitude of the consequences of opportunistic behavior. The opportunism is not simply detrimental; it is survival threatening. Where a sovereign task is involved, hidden action by the agent jeopardizes the system as a whole. Outlawing outsourcing the security task minimizes the chances of those with the guns using them for their own ends. The state will still face agency problems within its police and security forces, yet it is best equipped to

---

[41] Douglas North, John Wallis, and Barry Weingast, *Violence and Social Orders: A Conceptual Framework for Interpreting Recorded Human History* (Cambridge: Cambridge University Press, 2009), p. 169.

inculcate the ethics and professional responsibilities consistent with the implementation of sovereign tasks. Outsourcing security tasks to non-state armed groups is viewed as symptomatic of failed states, or perhaps as simply a historical phenomenon. Wilson observes that "the historically-minded among us will recall that at one time . . . nations went to war with mercenary armies."[42] But paid and unpaid armed bands still go to war for nations. Despite the theory and the clear security worries of weapons getting into the wrong hands, all sorts of governments in all sorts of states, both democratic and non-democratic, and in countries at different levels of development, continue to outsource violence. Governments remain willing to delegate even their original task.

Armed non-state actors on the side of governments flourish in today's and yesterday's wars.[43] They fight against Islamists in Nigeria. They seized Crimea for Russia. Teaming up with Sunni "Awakening" militias in Iraq provided force numbers for the American "surge" in 2007. In Afghanistan, the United States delegates security tasks to a variety of more or less reliable groups in order to save its own forces the time and trouble of delivering security. At the outset, these included Uzbek forces under General Dostum, who had his own interests and agenda. He reportedly let Taliban prisoners suffocate in the shipping containers in which they were held. According to a *Washington Post* report, the foreign principal attempted to assert control by "buzzing" Dostum with a B-1 bomber.[44] The Afghan

---

[42] James Q. Wilson, *Bureaucracy* (New York: Basic Books, 1989), pp. 346–348; Oliver E. Williamson, "Public and Private Bureaucracies: A Transaction Cost Economics Perspective," *The Journal of Law, Economics, and Organization* 15, no. 1 (1999): 322.

[43] Sabine Carey and I collected systematic global data on these groups showing that they are a standard component of the security sector. For the data: http://www.sabinecarey.com/militias. This discussion of the incentives for delegating to these groups draws on Sabine C. Carey and Neil J. Mitchell, "Progovernment Militias," *Annual Review of Political Science* 20 (2017): 127–147; Carey et al., "Governments, Informal Links to Militias, and Accountability," *Journal of Conflict Resolution* 59, no. 5 (2015): 76–80; "Risk Mitigation, Regime Security, and Militias: Beyond Coup-proofing," *International Studies Quarterly* 60, no. 1 (2016): 59–72; "States, the Security Sector, and the Monopoly of Violence: A New Database on Pro-Government Militias," *Journal of Peace Research* 50, no. 2 (2013): 249–258; Mitchell et al., "The Impact of Pro-Government Militias on Human Rights Violations," *International Interactions* 40, no. 5 (2014): 812–836.

[44] "Dostum, A Former Warlord Who Was Once America's Man in Afghanistan, May Be Back," *Washington Post*, April 23, 2014. https://www.washingtonpost.com/world/

Local Police (ALP) is the largest of the irregular armed groups used by the United States. Founded in 2010, it provides the agents necessary for a village-based defense force against the Taliban. It saves the time, effort and the lives of American soldiers. But its performance is mixed. The ALP kill fewer civilians than the Taliban and some of the other militias, but according to the International Crisis Group, the ALP members frequently abuse their authority for their private interest, which is flatly opposed to the interest of the United States. The ALP engages in extortion, kidnapping, and extrajudicial killings. Village elders nominate local men to serve, but selection and monitoring are a challenge: "When an elder from Wardak province complained in 2014 about a local ALP commander whose men were allegedly stealing from travellers, robbing houses and kidnapping teenage boys for sexual entertainment . . . ALP members tied his long beard to a rope and fastened it to their ALP pickup. 'They killed him by dragging,' a witness said." Some former Taliban are members of ALP: "These Taliban just shaved their beards. . . . Before they were stopping cars and ordering people to pray, but now they ask for money."[45] The International Crisis Group estimated that only one-third of the units were on task, yet if benchmarked against the Taliban or some other armed groups in the country, the ALP were the best available option for a disliked security task that the United States did not want to perform itself.

Vigilantes in Nigeria were the option chosen by the Nigerian government in 2013 in Borno state. This Civilian Joint Task Force (CJTF) was formed in the context of the inadequate response of regular forces to the terror created by Boko Haram and the kidnapping of hundreds of schoolgirls that sparked international outrage. As governments are unsure of these agents, they tend to be lightly armed, which makes them less effective.

dostum-a-former-warlord-who-was-once-americas-man-in-afghanistan-may-be-back/
2014/04/23/9d1a7670-c63d-11e3-8b9a-8e0977a24aeb_story.html.

[45] "The Future of the Afghan Local Police," *International Crisis Group*, June 4, 2015, pp. 10, 21.

The powerful incentives to delegate violence remain. Militias provide more personnel under arms in remote areas at less cost and they may help ensure against disloyalty in the regular forces. Delegating to irregular forces adds personnel to the government-side forces. It may also deprive the opponent of recruits. "Force multiplication" is a commonly identified incentive for delegation, but in a conflict force, "subtraction" might well be a calculation. In such a context, even with the necessary force strength, it may be useful to build in redundancy and delegate to some who may expend little effort for you, if only to ensure that their guns are not pointed at you.

Under some conditions, governments have disloyal agents within their regular forces and experience coups. The probity hazard may be at times greater in-house than outside. Governments may distrust the loyalty and rectitude of the regular forces. One choice is to place their confidence in militia forces. The government of Iran made this choice after the revolution in 1979. Alongside the regular forces, it positioned the extremists in the Revolutionary Guard and Basij militia. Finally, these agents, too, may multitask. An incentive discussed in Chapter 6 is that militia forces help manage the blame for more controversial uses of violence.

What about the win-loss record of militias and the consequences of deploying these armed groups? Using militia forces in the "surge" in Iraq provided breathing space to begin American disengagement. In Nigeria, the vigilantes pushed Boko Haram out of the city of Maiduguri in Borno State, and the use of vigilantes was then adopted in Cameroon and Chad. The adoption of the policy elsewhere suggests it was evaluated as a success. In Afghanistan, the "cheap but dangerous" ALP provide some security advantages, and even critical observers such as the International Crisis Group note that terminating the contract might lead ALP personnel to turn their guns to other uses.[46] As elsewhere, it is difficult to be precise about the contribution of the agent.

---

[46] *International Crisis Group* (2015), pp. i–ii.

8

Thinking about where to put the boundaries of delegation or how to draw the line between public and private sector, nothing seems to be indisputably in-house, from caring for loved ones to what theorists had thought were sovereign tasks. But some progress on the question is possible. It is worth asking whether the task has some inherent content for the principal. Her identity as a parent or a student may be wrapped up with writing an essay or encouraging a toddler to find a degree of independence. If the task has content of this sort for the principal, it is unlikely to be delegated. Second, in choosing what tasks to delegate and idiosyncrasies aside (Jimmy Carter and the tennis court), the relative importance of the task is a driver. The wisdom offered by sociologists such as Max Weber as well as some rational choice scholars about states seeking to monopolize violence makes sense theoretically if it lacks prima facie plausibility.[47] In extraordinary times, in insurgencies, with rebel groups threatening the survival of the state, then presumably the risks associated with delegating a sovereign task become more acceptable.

If the *Life and Adventures of Robinson Crusoe* is reliable, the urge to save time and effort is not simply rational. It is almost primal. Robinson, alone on his island, saw a man fleeing some very hungry cannibals: "It came now very warmly upon my thoughts, and indeed irresistibly, that now was my time to get a servant." At great risk to himself, he rescued the man. The first word he taught this man (the only human being he had encountered in twenty-five years on the island) was "master." At first, he was anxious about his new delegation relationship. It had been a hurried selection process and, naturally enough, he did not know whether he could trust the other party. He took various, fortunately unnecessary measures in order to guard against betrayal: "for never man had a more faithful, loving, sincere

---

[47] See, for example, North, Wallace and Weingast, *Violence and Social Orders: A Conceptual Framework for Interpreting Recorded Human History*; Robert Bates, *When Things Fell Apart: State Failure in Late Twentieth Century Africa* (Cambridge: Cambridge University Press, 2008).

servant than Friday was to me."[48] Robinson's relationship with Man Friday brought him happiness. When delegation is unhappy, it is so in familiar ways. Agents seek their private interests in the delegation relationship. Unlike Man Friday, taxi drivers, nursing home staff, football functionaries, supply chain manufacturers, kings, politicians, and warlords may not repay your trust. Monitoring them may not be easy, particularly with slack collective principals. Citizens, shareholders, or football team owners do not pay enough attention to what is being done in their name, and individual actors free-ride on the monitoring efforts of others. Or it may be too strict, inducing a high turnover of agents. Furthermore, outsourcing this task may not be easy either. Monitors themselves may need monitoring, and the principal may incur further agency costs and have to take other measures to offset the reputational risks of outsourcing to a textile factory in Bangladesh. The struggle for an information advantage between actors with different interests is at the heart of the relationship and central to the problem of control. We may try to anticipate eventualities and agree on things before entering the relationship, but as the surrogate contract illustrated, prior agreements do not guarantee a happy outcome.

Finally, you may be wondering about Tolstoy's Levin, whom we met toward the beginning of the chapter. How did he get out of his difficulties with his agricultural laborers with interests flatly opposed to his, and the task of overseeing them? The answer should be no surprise. He delegated the disliked task: "he handed over all the now revolting business of the estate to the bailiff, and set off next day to a remote district to see his friend Sviyazhsky."[49]

---

[48] Daniel Defoe, *The Life and Adventures of Robinson Crusoe* (London: MacMillan and Co., [1719] 1866), p. 212.
[49] Tolstoy (2012), p. 292.

3
Expertise

We delegate disliked tasks, although perhaps not as often as we should. We also delegate complex tasks, in order to harness specialized knowledge and skill for our benefit. The commissioning parents will need, in addition to the surrogate willing to put in the time and effort to carry the baby to term, the expertise of a doctor, a lawyer, and then, as they begin to put money aside for university fees, perhaps a financial expert as well. These experts belong to professions, which develop procedures to preserve their knowledge advantage and sustain their specialized work. By this measure, by our repeated delegation to these expert agents, delegation is successful.

But failure is worth analyzing. These agents do not always live up to their professional responsibilities. Of all agents, experts, in possession of specialized knowledge and skill, are best able to press home their advantage over the principal. I will first discuss how those looking after our finances or health resist monitoring, in order to help set up an in-depth analysis of a curious, institutionalized, theory-defying, and highly alarming pattern of behavior found in the Catholic Church and in the military. These may appear to be two unlikely institutions to put together. What they share is a failure to respond in a timely and proportionate way to problems with their agents.

1

When we delegate the task of looking after our financial health, often we do so uneasily. Is the agent competent or trustworthy? On the other hand, the option of not delegating and being left to tame

Why Delegate?. Neil J. Mitchell, Oxford University Press (2021). © Oxford University Press.
DOI: 10.1093/oso/9780190904197.003.0003

the bulls, bears, and animal spirits of the financial world on one's own seems perilous. Before asking someone to do this task, we try to tilt the balance of power in our favor. We screen for the skill and preferences of prospective agents. We want financial guidance from someone who understands the world of investment and who has our interests in mind. We might collect information from friends about how they manage their affairs. Country club conversations and high society networking famously built a very select clientele for Bernie Madoff to defraud.[1] Friends may have your trust, but not the knowledge to give you a good steer. Perhaps the most remarkable feature of this case is not the trust betrayed by Madoff. We expect individuals in this industry to be highly self-interested, stories of financial advisers letting us down are not uncommon, and fraud is an everyday occurrence. Nor is it the prominence of his victims, whether Hollywood actors or the owners of the New York Mets. They have the money. What is noteworthy is the woeful performance of the regulatory agency charged with monitoring for Madoff-type opportunism.

Madoff's story is well known and quickly told. His scheme depended on the client-principal's fear of the complexity of the financial world. With billions of dollars involved, Madoff claimed a year-on-year market-beating performance. He supposedly implemented a "split strike conversion strategy." Such a strategy protects an investment in shares against market downturns using options to sell or buy at specified prices. His claims were not credible to those in the know. The impressive sounding strategy could limit losses, but it could not produce the consistent gains that Madoff claimed. Actually, he was using new investors to pay older investors. He lured in investors, including members of European royal families, by appearing hard to get and then giving them status as "special" customers.[2] This "Ponzi"

---

[1] "Madoff Victims, Five Years the Wiser," *New York Times*, December 7, 2013. https://www.nytimes.com/2013/12/08/business/madoff-victims-five-years-the-wiser.html.

[2] Harry Markopolos, Testimony before the United States House of Representatives Committee on Financial Services, February 4, 2009, p. 12; Securities and Exchange Commission, Office of Investigations. Investigation of Failure of the SEC to Uncover Bernard Madoff's Ponzi Scheme. Report No. OIG-509 (2009), p. 21. https://www.sec.gov/news/studies/2009/oig-509.pdf.

scheme came unstuck with the financial crisis and when investors wanted their money. Madoff pleaded guilty to fraud charges and was sentenced to 150 years. The information advantage held by Madoff over his clients was the key to his success in getting them to invest. As a whistle-blower described it: "He knew most wouldn't understand it and would be embarrassed to admit their ignorance."[3] He emphasized the complexity of the task.

What of the institution watching over these relationships? The Securities and Exchange Commission (SEC) staff are supposed to understand these schemes, to compensate for the information asymmetry, and to provide a safeguard against rogue agents. The SEC received repeated warnings about Bernie Madoff. But in this case the agent held an information advantage over the monitors as well. The SEC staff lacked the experience and acumen for the job. They could not grasp the implausibility of Madoff's claims about the consistent and substantial gains he made. They did not respond appropriately to the early warnings provided by individuals and in the press.

The very visible failure of the SEC led to a lengthy self-examination. The SEC's Office of Investigations Report, "Investigation of Failure of the SEC to Uncover Bernard Madoff's Ponzi Scheme," recognized that red flags went up years earlier, including the SEC's own inadequate 1992 investigation into another company with which Madoff was associated. Ironically, the whistle-blowing prompting this watchdog's superficial inquiries, which produced findings of no fraud, served Madoff to reassure and secure new investors: he had been vetted by the SEC.

The SEC's investigation of itself suggests that responsibility lay with insufficiently expert staff, not collusion. The case led to a recognition of the need for lawyers to improve their training in the industry they were regulating.[4] Delegating to Madoff, an agent with a claim to specialist knowledge, was an inadequately examined route to misery. Indeed, a badly trained watchdog led individuals down this route.

[3] Markopolos (2009), 6.
[4] See Robert Rhee, "The Madoff Scandal. Market Regulatory Failure and the Business Education of Lawyers," *The Journal of Corporation Law* 35, no. 2 (2009): 363–392.

2

Financial health perhaps leads to physical health. Medical expertise may have a price, yet the good news is that in normal times in the United States the insured see a doctor relatively quickly. The average wait for elective surgery is considerably shorter than in the United Kingdom. The bad news is that where you or your insurance company pay these agents by the service that they provide rather than on a salary basis, you may be somewhat less satisfied with your encounter with a doctor: 20 percent of Americans surveyed felt their doctor had recommended a treatment without benefit, in comparison to 10 percent in the United Kingdom.[5]

Despite the underlying medical science, there is variation among countries in the frequency with which procedures are performed. Hysterectomy rates are higher in the United States than elsewhere. A woman in the United States is about twice as likely to have a hysterectomy than in other similarly developed countries, and she is likely to undergo this procedure at an earlier age. If you have a coronary issue in the United States, the evidence suggests you are more likely to have surgery than in Britain or Germany.[6]

International comparisons are complicated, but the organization of healthcare and in particular the financial arrangements you make with the agent-healthcare provider appear to affect the delivery of treatment. In China, healthcare specialists profit from prescribing antibiotics and giving injections; they prescribe and inject at higher rates than elsewhere.[7] A "fee for service" payment system encourages the over-provision of treatment, especially where costs are passed to insurers. Dr. Steven Schroeder and former Senate Majority Leader

---

[5] Alan M. Garber and Jonathan Skinner. "Is American Health Care Uniquely Inefficient?" *Journal of Economic Perspectives* 22, no. 4 (2008): 34

[6] See Kim McPherson, Giorgia Gon, and Maggie Scott, "International Variations in a Selected Number of Surgical Procedures," *OECD Health Working Papers* 61 (2013): 22; Garber and Skinner (2008), 587.

[7] Yongbin Li, Jing Xu Fang Wang, Bin Wang, et al., "Overprescribing in China, Driven by Financial Incentives, Results in Very High Use of Antibiotics, Injections, and Corticosteroids," *Health Affairs* 31, no. 5 (2012): 1075–1082.

William Frist argue for the phasing out of fee-for-service payments.[8] Despite its high spending on healthcare, the United States receives, at best, average returns in terms of the overall health of its population. Life expectancy at birth was better in over thirty other countries in 2015, according to the United Nations Human Development Report. The evidence suggests that separating compensation from the number of treatments performed or drugs prescribed reduces goal conflict between these agents and those who seek to benefit from their efforts.

Medical students may have large bills to pay. Many choose well-paying specialties (anesthesiology, radiology, and ophthalmology) that offer a more regular working week, as Harvard Medical School professors Pamela Hartzband and Jerome Groopman describe. The "money culture," they argue, can interfere with professional responsibility and distorts the practice of medicine. One feature of healthcare in the United States is the number of high-earning specialists in comparison to primary care doctors and the ease with which the ill-informed refer themselves to specialists. Knowing enough to select a competent and properly motivated agent makes for successful delegation. There is also the concern that financial incentives and pressures demotivate medical professionals. Hartzband and Groopman argue that in the United States, the tradition of community-mindedness is under threat from the money culture.[9] These scholars suggest that the place that financial incentives now occupy harms not only the patient, but also the ethically motivated and professionally responsible agent. It detracts from the expected non-monetary benefits of work experience and any ideals about the medical profession that give this agent a special identity and make this work intrinsically rewarding. We saw in the previous chapter that for a principal, a task that somehow defines her may create a barrier to delegation. For an agent, when the task has some inherent

[8] Steven A. Schroeder and William Frist, "Phasing Out Fee-For-Service Payment," *New England Journal of Medicine* 368 (2013): 2029–2032.

[9] Hartzband and Groopman, "Money and the Changing Culture of Medicine," *The New England Journal of Medicine* 360 (2009): 102; see also Hartzband and Groopman,"How to Fix Our Health Care System," *New York Review of Books* 64 (July 2017): 47–50.

connection with his identity and self-esteem, then the task may get done well, even in the absence of powerful external incentives or close monitoring.

As the Nobel economist Kenneth Arrow observed, in many ways the physician-patient relationship is exemplary for principal-agent theory. Information asymmetry is severe, with the patient-principal unable to monitor the doctor-agent. Contracts are complex and incomplete given the necessity of wide agent discretion and the uncertainty of outcomes. All the same and despite the latitude for shirking, patients keep delegating. According to Arrow, the explanation for this puzzle lies "within the terms of principal-agent logic but in a way that *points beyond the usual bounds of economic analysis* [my italics]." Arrow suggests that the standard principal-agent assumption of narrowly self-interested agents does not apply so well to the medical profession. Instead, the agent is trusted because of a higher purpose at work. These agents are guided by a norm of professional responsibility, which, Arrow says, "is clearly enforced in good measure by systems of ethics, internalized during the education process and enforced in some measure by formal punishments and more broadly by reputations."[10] While with Madoff we might expect the agent to be self-interested in an uncomplicated way, with more idealistic professions self-interest has "social" as well as economic content. We expect codes of conduct to matter more, monitoring to matter less, and agents to be motivated by the task itself. The trust in the agent and in her professionalism, afforded by the principal, may be motivation in itself. Such an agent, which economists George Akelof and Rachel Kranton describe as an "insider," identifies with the organization and will derive some satisfaction from the task itself, lowering the need for monetary incentives.[11] These agents gain some benefit from carrying out the principal's task efficiently, some sense of self-worth beyond any monetary benefits the role provides. With this

---

[10] Kenneth J. Arrow, "The Economics of Agency," in *Principals and Agents: The Structure of Business*, edited by John W. Pratt and Richard Zeckhauser (Boston: Harvard Business School Press, 1985), 50; Arrow, "Uncertainty and the Welfare Economics of Medical Care," *The American Economic Review* 53, no. 5 (1963): 941–973.

[11] George A. Akerlof and Rachel E. Kranton, *Identity Economics: How Our Identities Shape Our Work, Wages, and Well-Being* (Princeton, NJ: Princeton University Press, 2010), 42.

type of agent, there is a risk that "external" financial incentives (the money culture in American medical practice) may even displace or "crowd out" a spirit of obligation and service. Developing empirical tests of this crowding-out effect is challenging. Economists Imran Rasul and Daniel Rogger's study of the Nigerian civil service suggests that allowing agent discretion and relying on multitasking bureaucrats' professionalism, as opposed to using incentives and monitoring, have positive effects on project completion rates without leading to more corruption.[12] Work by political scientists underlines the importance of professionalism in delegation relationships.[13] Yet what remains beyond the usual bounds of principal-agent analysis is the particular complexity of addressing wrongdoing when it is done by these higher-purpose professionals.

Early in the development of principal-agent theory, Arrow recognized that professions can self-regulate and develop nonmarket solutions such as codes of ethics to improve performance. But when the code breaks, these professionals present tenacious control problems. Despite Arrow's assertion about ethics that are internalized during the education process and the presence of formal and reputational enforcement, in the real world it is surprisingly difficult to enforce this professional responsibility with formal punishments. He underestimated the difficulty of enforcement. The reason is that these agents have the capacity to make punishment highly costly to the principal.

As for reputation, if anything, a concern for reputation has the opposite effect of that envisioned. It motivates covering up the misdeed, not living up to the expected standards of conduct. When professional responsibility fails to keep these agents in line, the perceived

Avinash Dixit, "Incentives and Organizations in the Public Sector: An Interpretative Review," *The Journal of Human Resources* 37, no. 4 (2002): 696–727. Dixit points out organizations may foster esprit de corps and "in reality, agents may get utility from some aspects of the task itself" (p. 714); Roland Bénabou and Jean Tirole, "Intrinsic and Extrinsic Motivation," *Review of Economic Studies* 70, no. 3 (2003): 489–520.

[12] Imran Rasul and Daniel Rogger, "Management of Bureaucrats and Public Service Delivery: Evidence from the Nigerian Civil Service," *The Economic Journal* 128 (2018): 413–446.

[13] For example, Brehm and Gates (1997); Miller and Whitford (2015).

costs of trying to redress the balance and monitor and punish the agents who depart from good practice are high. To uncover the process that encourages unexpected passivity in the principal, we can start with the medical profession, before moving to the religious and military examples.

In England, a doctor overdiagnosed and under-treated patients. A large number of women, fearful of breast cancer, received operations they did not need and which did them no good. The doctor inflated his patients' cancer risks and misrepresented the surgical procedure. He described his technique as a "cleavage sparing mastectomy," which did not go deep enough to deal with the problem for those with cancer.[14] Beyond the harm of surgery, those without cancer endured the stress of thinking they had it or would get it. Those with cancer had an ineffective treatment and a higher risk of recurrence. The surgeon was convicted of "wounding with intent" and was sentenced to a lengthy prison term. Even after the trial, it was difficult to know the nature of the private goods sought by this doctor that had interfered so catastrophically with his sense of professional responsibility. The prosecution argued that he did not act in the interests of the patient, pointed to money as well as to more "obscure motives," and speculated about a "God complex."[15] While motives may be difficult to isolate precisely, the theoretically important point is that there was some private gratification sought by the agent at the expense of the principal. He used his enormous information advantage over the principal to obtain that gratification. The National Health Service and the private hospitals where he performed operations paid millions in compensation. Even with the potential liabilities involved, these institutions had failed to respond appropriately to red flags. The surgeon had been suspended in 1996 and one or two colleagues sounded the alarm as early as 2003, but he operated until 2011.

---

[14] Professor Sir Ian Kennedy, "Review of the Response of Heart of England NHS Foundation Trust to Concerns about Mr. Ian Paterson's Surgical Practice" (2013), p. 4. https://hgs.uhb.nhs.uk/wp-content/uploads/Kennedy-Report-Final.pdf.

[15] "Breast Surgeon Ian Paterson 'Invented Cancer Risks,'" BBC, February 28, 2017. https://www.bbc.co.uk/news/uk-england-birmingham-39114317.

Ruined lives apart, four features of the case are of note. First, as Arrow observed, the knowledge gap characteristic of principal-agent relationships is wide in the patient-physician relationship, requiring a large leap of trust. Second, financial incentives are a powerful driver of agent behavior, but, as Arrow observed, they are not the only driver. Third, there was a lack of timely response to this rogue agent and the enforcement of professional responsibility. While there were whistle-blowers, other agents went along. Fourth, reputation effects encouraged secrecy, not correction of this behavior. In the National Health Service review of the case by Professor Sir Ian Kennedy, the executive summary pointed to these problems: "It is a story of clinicians going along with what they knew to be poor performance. It is a story of weak and indecisive leadership from senior managers. It is a story of secrecy and containment. It is a story of a Board which did not carry out its responsibilities. It is a story of a surgeon who chose on occasions to operate on women in a way unrecognised by his peers and thereby exposed them to harm."[16] Recruitment pressures and a shortage of breast surgeons was also a factor. He was an agent who was difficult to replace. As we shall see, some of the most serious and disturbing problems we face today share important features with this case. These problems come down to managing difficult-to-replace rogue agents who have specialized training and skills, others going along, secrecy, and weak leadership.

3

Two quite different organizations, dedicated to higher purposes, tolerate shocking agent opportunism. Around the world and for who knows how long, Catholic priests have avoided the consequences for their reckless and atrocious behavior. From Vietnam to Afghanistan, soldiers in usually well-disciplined armies, which pride themselves on adherence to the laws of war, escape punishment for war crimes. How does the search for salvation or security come to this?

---

[16] Kennedy (2013), p. 3.

The crimes of priests and soldiers appear to be unrelated phenomena. In their missions, in the types of individuals they attract to serve, and in the cloistered versus conflict-related violence that is perpetrated, they seem to present quite different problems. However, they come together as a puzzle within delegation theory. A useful theory points to, as well as solves, puzzles. As agent opportunism is at the principal's expense, the theory leads us to expect that those in charge will respond and impose penalties or dismiss the agent in order to put a stop to opportunism. What is puzzling across both these organizational contexts is the principal's systematic unwillingness to punish criminal noncompliance. So what explains the passivity?

It is not that the stakes are low. There could be no more flagrant violations of the authority vested in these agents. It is hard to imagine actions more contrary to the professional responsibility, specialized training, and education provided to these agents than the killing and humiliation of noncombatants or the abuse of the most vulnerable in their flock. If any noncompliance requires exemplary punishment for the misuse of the authority granted, it is for this violence and abuse, which is done for some perhaps obscure private benefit. Furthermore, the noncompliance of these agents costs the church or the taxpayers in the substantial compensation payments to victims and it is damaging to the institutional missions, if those are about winning and not losing hearts, minds, and souls.

Despite the expectation of professional responsibilities being clearly enforced by some measure of formal punishment, the strategy of those in charge has been to assist the agent in keeping his hidden actions hidden. Both sides of the delegation relationship in both organizations see this response as to their advantage. In that sense, a lack of enforcement is self-enforcing in this relationship. Both clerical and military hierarchies, in the United States and elsewhere, display a reluctance to investigate allegations of abuse and to punish and terminate the service of pedophile priests and war criminals, as principal-agent theory or just common decency would predict. This reluctance is not confined to one or two isolated cases.

Perhaps the claim about the passivity of those in the hierarchy of the Catholic Church will be more readily accepted than the claim regarding those in the hierarchy of Western, rule-of-law, civilian-led militaries. The church's failure attracted headline-grabbing external investigations from around the world, showing that wherever the church built its institutions, it had clerics working in them who were evading accountability for wrongdoing. The size of the scandal created by the church and the numbers of perpetrators and victims are on a different scale from that of the army. That said, the conduct of US and British military personnel and the response of those in charge have attracted the attention of the international community. A United Nations investigation by its Special Rapporteur on Extrajudicial, Summary or Arbitrary Executions and the authorization of an investigation into alleged war crimes by US soldiers (and Afghan and Taliban forces) in Afghanistan by the prosecutor of the International Criminal Court are evidence of something awry with military justice. If the numbers caught up in the wrongdoing differ between the church and the army, when it comes to understanding how those in charge respond, I argue that there is a common process at work.

The logic of delegation, with some modifications, helps us understand these apparently unrelated problems. The story is about how a principal manages *multiple* agents (not just the single agent found in some game theoretic models) with specialized knowledge and training, and the advantages that rogue agents extract from their privileged positions. Some examples will serve to illustrate the nature of agent opportunism in the two organizations.

4

A child in 1950s Australia, Max (not his real name) was nine when placed in the Hospitallers of St John of God Brothers Training Home for Retarded Boys. Once or twice a week over seven years, he was sexually and physically abused by the Brethren. After a year, Max told a doctor about his suffering. In retribution, a Hospitaller broke the boy's arm. Forty years later, Max reported the abuse to Broken Rites Australia, an organization that investigates sexual abuse in the Catholic Church, and to the police. The church compensated him financially.[17]

Denis (not his real name) had an intellectual disability and went to the St John of God Brothers home when he was seven. His disability got in the way of informing on his tormentors. The acts they performed on Denis were literally unspeakable.

During his weekends at home, Denis would wake screaming from nightmares and he often insisted on sleeping under the bed. He developed overtly sexualised behaviour and habits. . . . His siblings said they now felt guilty that they hadn't known or suspected anything was amiss. "We saw the behaviour but we didn't ever link it to being [sexually abused]," Carly said. "And I think one of the issues is that people with disabilities, when they display those behaviours, it is seen as being part of the disability."[18]

Only in the 1990s did the family establish what had happened to Denis. He named the six Brothers who had abused him. The church paid him compensation.

A 2017 Australian government-initiated inquiry into child sexual abuse revealed the scale of the problem. Victims suffered in 964 different Catholic institutions at the hands of 1,880 perpetrators (Catholic institutions accounted for 62 percent of the victims, Anglican institutions for 15 percent, followed by the Salvation Army at 7 percent). To describe it as "institutional abuse" is less useful, at least if it lifts responsibility from the perpetrators. The abuse was done by individuals who took advantage of what the institutional context offered them and who were protected by individuals above them in the chain of delegation who saw an advantage in doing so.

[17] Royal Commission Into Institutional Responses to Child Sexual Abuse (2017). https://www.childabuseroyalcommission.gov.au/narratives/max-deans-story.
[18] Royal Commission into Institutional Responses to Child Sexual Abuse (2017). https://www.childabuseroyalcommission.gov.au/narratives/carlys-story.

As Max's and Denis's stories illustrate, given the age of the victims, the nature of the abuse, and the outward respectability of the perpetrators, under-reporting is likely. Victims averaged ten years old when first targeted. In Australia, about 7 percent of priests were alleged to have committed abuse between 1950 and 2010. But in some of the Catholic residential institutions, the frequency of abuse among members of these institutions was much higher. For the Hospitallers of St John of God, with especially vulnerable children in their care, 40 percent of that religious community are alleged to have committed abuse.[19] This variation in abuse is partly a function of the amount of access to vulnerable children afforded by the type of institution.

The Australian findings fit a global pattern. In the United States in August 2018, a Pennsylvania grand jury found that over 300 priests were likely to have abused children. Most of the victims were boys and the authorities covered up the abuse.[20] This investigation, like the Australian inquiry, points to the passivity of the principal.

In February 2019, the church defrocked the Archbishop of Washington, DC, Cardinal Theodore McCarrick, for sexual abuse. Over decades, his misconduct was documented in allegations made to the Pope's representative in Washington, among others. These allegations, and the compensation paid to those who suffered at his hands, did not get in the way of McCarrick's career and elevation to cardinal in 2000.[21] McCarrick abused boys and men, notably those training for the priesthood. The abuse of children captures attention for understandable reasons, but there is also widespread abuse of vulnerable adults, including those in the service of the church.

In theory, we expect that when the alarm sounds for agent misconduct, the principal punishes. Furthermore, if we find that immediate superiors in the chain of delegation assisted in concealing

---

[19] Royal Commission into Institutional Responses to Child Sexual Abuse, Final Report (2017): p. 45.

[20] 40th Statewide Investigating Grand Jury, Report 1 (August 2018), p. 1. http://media-downloads.pacourts.us/InterimRedactedReportandResponses.pdf?cb=42148.

[21] "He Preyed on Men Who Wanted to Be Priests. Then He Became a Cardinal," *New York Times*, July 16, 2018. https://www.nytimes.com/2018/07/16/us/cardinal-mccarrick-abuse-priest.html.

misconduct, then we expect them to be punished. What we observe is that they go unpunished. Indeed, this wrongdoing did not get in the way of promotion. Only the very belated external pressure of government investigations produced some accountability. Pope followed pope, but the Vatican kept what it knew of the abuse to itself. Pope Francis, a popular and reformist pope elected by the College of Cardinals in 2013, shares his predecessors' reluctance to address this issue. The Australian Royal Commission asked the Vatican for documents on the conduct of Australian priests: "the Holy See responded, on 1 July 2014, that it was 'neither possible nor appropriate to provide the information requested.'"[22] Secrecy is policy. At the diocese level, the Pennsylvania grand jury found that the church's Code of Canon Law required bishops to keep secret archives for abuse complaints. The grand jury said the church had a "playbook for concealing the truth" from the police and the community. They employed euphemisms for sexual misconduct and violence, provided token treatment in church-run treatment centers, and relocated perpetrators.[23] A similar pattern was found in Germany. Sixty percent of abusive priests got away without punishment, with many abusers simply transferred to different parishes.[24] The shared pattern of abuse implicates the hierarchy. The Australian Royal Commission pointed to "catastrophic failures of leadership of Catholic Church authorities over many decades."[25] Abusers continued to perform tasks for the church, perhaps in a different location, and retained access to children.

The catastrophic failure of leadership outlasts individual leaders. In 2014 in response to the public outcry, Pope Francis appointed a Pontifical Commission for the Protection of Minors. Within three years, the two victim members of the Commission had resigned in

---

[22] "4,444 Victims: Extent of Abuse in Catholic Church in Australia Revealed," *The Guardian*, February 6, 2017. https://www.theguardian.com/australia-news/2017/feb/06/4444-victims-extent-of-abuse-in-catholic-church-in-australia-revealed.

[23] 40th Statewide Investigating Grand Jury, Report 1 (2018), p. 3.

[24] "Shocking Sexual Abuse of Children by German Clergy Detailed in Report," *The Guardian*, September 25, 2018. https://www.theguardian.com/world/2018/sep/25/report-details-sexual-abuse-german-catholic-church.

[25] Royal Commission (2017), p. 61.

frustration with the process. The Pontifical Commission appeared to be a fig leaf for the church.[26] The Pope's 2018 visit to Chile provoked protests. He had appointed a bishop, Bishop Barrios, who was known to have covered up for a repeat abuser. The Pope tried denial. He labeled the claims of abuse "calumnies."[27] Noting that bishops still do not have to report allegations of sexual abuse to the police unless the country's laws require it, the *Economist* said of the Pope: "the biggest mystery surrounding this man, who combines toughness and compassion, is why he has not applied his rough-house tactics to the issue that most cries out for action: clerical sex abuse."[28] This man behaved as others in his position always have behaved. The mystery for the principal-agent theorist is not that selfish individuals the world over exploit the authority granted them for some form of private gain. That is assumed. The biggest mystery is why they are able to continue to do it. And why do we find a similar pattern of behavior among those in charge when faced with agent misconduct in another highly hierarchical organization?

5

In September 2011 in Helmand province in Afghanistan, a British Royal Marine shot dead a wounded Afghan man. He offered the departed some last words: "Shuffle off this mortal coil, you cunt." The marine told his comrades: "Obviously this doesn't go anywhere, fellas. . . . I've just broken the Geneva convention."[29] It did

[26] "Abuse Survivor Quits Vatican's Child Protection Panel," *BBC*, March 1, 2017. https://www.bbc.co.uk/news/world-europe-39125191.

[27] "Sex Crimes in Chile: Ghosts from the Past," *The Economist*, July 28, 2018. https://www.economist.com/the-americas/2018/07/28/chiles-catholic-church-faces-new-charges-of-sexual-abuse; "Pope Francis on Chile Sexual Abuse Scandal: 'I Was Part of the Problem.'" *The Guardian*, May 2, 2018. https://www.theguardian.com/world/2018/may/02/pope-francis-chile-sexual-abuse-scandal-part-of-problem.

[28] "Is the Pope Catholic?," *The Economist*, March 18, 2017. https://www.economist.com/international/2017/03/16/francis-is-facing-down-opposition-from-traditionalists-and-vatican-bureaucrats.

[29] "Military Court Releases Audio of Moment Marine Sergeant Shot Afghan," *The Guardian*, November 7, 2013. https://www.theguardian.com/uk-news/2013/nov/07/military-court-audio-marine-shot-afghan.

go somewhere—only as a result of the accidental discovery of the helmet camera video of the incident during a police (not military) investigation of an entirely different crime. The marine was convicted for murder, reduced to manslaughter on appeal. He served a three-and-half-year prison term.

It may seem a light sentence. Yet the surprising aspect of this case was that any time was served. It was the marine's bad luck that the video and audio evidence fell into the hands of external authorities in the form of the ordinary police. Routinely, our own troops' war crimes go uninvestigated and unpunished. Of all armies, those responsible to civilian leaders in mature liberal democracies like the United States or the United Kingdom should be most likely to discipline those who kill or torture noncombatants. One of the most stable findings in global studies of human rights violations is that these mature democracies have a much better record of protecting human rights than any other type of political regime.[30] But when violations occur, those in charge systematically fail to deliver accountability. For evidence, we can draw on the work of military historians.

The historian, Sir Max Hastings writes, "during and after the Second World War, scarcely any Allied soldiers, sailors or airmen were prosecuted for war crimes, though there was ample evidence to support charges, had there been the will to pursue them."[31] For the My Lai massacre in Vietnam, in which hundreds of unarmed villagers were killed and many women raped, one soldier was punished. The punishment of Lieutenant Calley was not the result of superiors in the chain of command responding in a timely and appropriate way. It was a result of external investigative reporting and a motivated congressman. Even so, three years of house arrest does not seem to fit the atrocity that had been committed.

---

[30] For example, Todd Landman, *Human Rights and Democracy: The Precarious Triumph of Ideals* (London: Bloomsbury, 2013); on the types of democratic elections that are protective of human rights, see David L. Cingranelli and Mikhail Filippov, "Electoral Rules and Incentives to Protect Human Rights," *Journal of Politics* 72, no. 1 (2010): 243–257.

[31] Max Hastings, "Wrath of the Centurions," *London Review of Books*, January 25, 2018: 19–22.

In May 1970, an American soldier wrote to Chief of Staff, General Westmoreland, to tell him of "things as bad as My Lay." He did not tell a congressman as he did not want to "hurt the army." In our terms, the soldier assumed that the control failure stemmed from information asymmetry. Alerting those in charge to opportunism is what is normally required for them to reassert control. In part, the whistle-blower blamed the bad things on the "body count" metric used as a measure of success for battalion commanders and for the award of medals to snipers. As Napoleon said, it is with baubles that men are led, and as we know from the New York police force and the gearing of performance to the number of tickets that they issued, numerical targets command an agent's attention and can create perverse incentives. Body counts created incentives to shoot Vietnamese civilians. Snipers set sunrise ambushes for rice farmers on the way to the paddy field: "I mean *lots* of Vietnamese got killed this way. . . . If I am only 10 percent right, and believe me its lots more, then I am trying to tell you about 120–150 murders, or a My Lay each month for over a year."[32] The Pulitzer Prize–winning book by Deborah Nelson, *The War behind Me: Vietnam Veterans Confront the Truth about U.S. War Crimes*, used the testimony of hundreds of soldiers held in declassified archives to document the killing and torture perpetrated by US forces, which included waterboarding, electrical shocks to the genitals, and rape.

The Nixon administration knew the allegations of war crimes were true, yet it was Vietnam veteran John Kerry and other whistle-blowing veterans that were to have their loyalty and credibility questioned. Information about agent misconduct was available, but the principal did not respond as expected. As Max Hastings describes the response to My Lai: "the consistent behaviour of all the officers in the chain of command, and later by officers in Washington, helped dismiss claims of a major war crime for many months."[33] Those up the chain of delegation tried to keep the agents' actions hidden.

---

[32] Deborah Nelson, *The War behind Me: Vietnam Veterans Confront the Truth about U.S. War Crimes* (New York: Basic Books, 2008): p. 78.

[33] Hastings (2018), p. 21.

There may have been lessons that were learned from Vietnam, but not about holding perpetrators of war crimes to account. In Iraq and Afghanistan, and irrespective of what military is involved, the preference of commanders is to keep their agents' violations hidden. Both American and British forces fail to investigate and punish such opportunism. Early in the Iraq campaign, the *Washington Post* drew attention to the issue with a piece titled "Homicide Charges Rare in Iraq War; Few Troops Tried for Killing Civilians."[34] One former British officer and lawyer observed that in Afghanistan, "there is little oversight. . . . Not a single prosecution has resulted from the many dozens of civilian casualties inflicted by British forces."[35] While the prospect of compensation generates false or "vexatious" claims, as British Prime Minister Theresa May described them, by December 2016, compensation totaling 22 million pounds had been paid by the United Kingdom Ministry of Defence in 331 out-of-court settlements.[36]

There are recent allegations against members of elite Special Forces units from the United States, the United Kingdom, and Australia operating in Afghanistan. None has been properly investigated at the time of writing. A US Special Forces unit is alleged to have tortured and murdered civilians. The Afghan government demanded the withdrawal of the unit. A journalist, Mattieu Aikens, who interviewed witnesses and others, writes that "even after the bodies started turning up, U.S. officials continued to deny any responsibility."[37] No prosecutions followed.[38] The United States did reopen an inquiry into the case in 2015, but has provided no further information.

[34] *Washington Post*, August 28, 2006. https://www.washingtonpost.com/archive/politics/2006/08/28/homicide-charges-rare-in-iraq-war-span-classbankheadfew-troops-tried-for-killing-civiliansspan/04a88326-c54c-4e2b-9ce7-501723f834a3/.

[35] Frank Ledwidge, *Losing Small Wars: British Military Failure in Iraq and Afghanistan* (New Haven, CT: Yale University Press 2012), p. 186.

[36] "British Troops Breach the Geneva Convention in Iraq, High Court Rules," *Guardian*, 14 December 2017. https://www.theguardian.com/world/2017/dec/14/british-troops-breached-geneva-conventions-in-iraq-high-court-rules.

[37] Mattieu Aikens, "The A-Team Killings," *Rolling Stone*, November 6, 2013. https://www.rollingstone.com/interactive/feature-a-team-killings-afghanistan-special-forces/.

[38] Amnesty International, *Left in The Dark: Failures of Accountability for Civilian Casualties Caused By International Military Operations in Afghanistan* (London: Amnesty International, 2014), p. 10. https://www.amnesty.org.nz/left-dark-failures-accountability-civilian-casualties-caused-international-military-operations.

For its part, the United Kingdom has abandoned its inquiry into allegations that its elite Special Air Service (SAS) personnel killed unarmed Afghan civilians and falsified reports between 2010 and 2013.[39] It was alleged that the soldiers had Russian pistols to plant on those they killed, turning noncombatants into combatants. Carrying "a drop weapon" is a practice used by American and Australian Special Forces as well. There is an interchange of personnel between these units helping to explain the diffusion of this practice. The British government did initiate an inquiry called Operation Northmoor into the allegations in 2014. Then they worried that it would damage public trust. They shut it down. There was a desire in the Ministry of Defence "to just make it go away."[40] One Afghan mother received an "assistance payment" (not "compensation" to avoid an admission of responsibility) from the British government for the killing of three sons. They were allegedly shot by the SAS.

There remains an Antipodean hope for accountability. *Human Rights Watch* researcher Patricia Gossman describes Australia's elite forces reportedly killing an unarmed elderly man "in an initiation ritual" and other war crimes, notes the US and UK failures in investigating their forces activities, and wonders, "Will Australia Provide Justice for Afghanistan War Crimes?"[41] An Australian judge is investigating these cases.

In 2017, the British government also shut down its inquiry into "historical cases" from the Iraq war. The only British conviction for unlawful killing in Iraq is for beating to death a hotel receptionist, Baha Mousa, during the weekend he spent in British custody. One

---

[39] "SAS Allies Hit by Claims of Unlawful Killing," *Sunday Times*, July 16, 2017. https://www.thetimes.co.uk/article/sas-allies-hit-by-claims-of-unlawful-killing-8qp97kvtb.

[40] "Revealed: How the Inquiry Was 'Made to Go Away,'" *Sunday Times*, July 2, 2017. https://www.thetimes.co.uk/article/revealed-how-inquiry-into-sas-unit-accused-of-executing-civilians-was-made-to-go-away-investigation-kill-killing-mod-ministry-defence-xt0mszl0k; "'Rogue' SAS Unit Accused of Executing Unarmed Civilians," *Sunday Times*, July 2, 2017. https://www.thetimes.co.uk/article/rogue-sas-unit-accused-of-executing-civilians-in-afghanistan-f2bqlc897.

[41] *Human Rights Watch* (June 20, 2018). https://www.hrw.org/news/2018/06/20/will-australia-provide-justice-afghanistan-war-crimes; see also "The Afghan Files," ABC. July 10, 2017. https://www.abc.net.au/news/2017-07-11/killings-of-unarmed-afghans-by-australian-special-forces/8466642.

soldier received a twelve-month sentence for "inhumane treatment." Shutting down the inquiry did not stop investigative reporters from the *Sunday Times* and the *BBC* getting access to a secret archive of more than 300 statements and documents testifying to the routine abuse and sexual humiliation of Iraqis by, for example, the soldiers of Scotland's renowned Black Watch Regiment. The commanding officer was notified of the abusive behavior of the soldiers by the regimental chaplain. It did not protect a taxi driver and a teacher, picked up on faulty intelligence, and reportedly beaten to death.[42] The British record is disappointing given that the Blair government, which sent the troops to Iraq and Afghanistan, had announced an "ethical foreign policy" and claimed to make human rights a cornerstone of the administration. It demonstrates the power of the forces that shape this delegation relationship, making hypocrites of democratic leaders, doubtless well-intentioned at the time. Sincerely stated commitments give way to the strong incentives not to enforce professional responsibilities in these organizational contexts.

In 2009, a United Nations Special Rapporteur on Extrajudicial, Summary or Arbitrary Executions noted that while there was no evidence that United States forces were committing "widespread intentional killings of civilians," at the same time there had been "chronic and deplorable accountability failures with respect to policies, practices and conduct that resulted in alleged unlawful killings." He drew the government's attention to a soldier who received a reprimand, a two-month confinement to base, and a fine for the "negligent homicide" of an Iraqi general who naively had turned himself in. The UN Rapporteur noted, "I have received no response."[43] In contrast, the Holy See responds, if just to say it is not "possible or appropriate" to provide the information requested. From President Richard Nixon to Prime Minister Boris Johnson (who reportedly sacked his Northern Ireland Secretary in February 2020 for agreeing

[42] "Revealed: The Evidence of War Crimes Ministers Tried to Bury," *Sunday Times*, November 17, 2019. https://www.thetimes.co.uk/article/revealed-the-evidence-of-war-crimes-ministers-tried-to-bury-6x2fb63ts.

[43] United Nations General Assembly, *Report of the Special Rapporteur on Extrajudicial, Summary or Arbitrary Executions No. A/HRC/11/2/Add.5* (May 28, 2009), p. 25

to the prosecution of soldiers for violations during the 1970s and 1980s in Northern Ireland), democratic politicians are reluctant to allow the investigation and punishment of war crimes, even when they gain no strategic advantage from these crimes and when the numbers of soldiers implicated are relatively few in comparison to the numbers deployed and to the misconduct perpetrated by the armies of non-democracies. Indeed, instead of shutting down inquiries, one might expect these politicians to take the opportunity presented to enforce Arrow's professional responsibility, to demonstrate in an exemplary way the power of the rule of law and the high discipline and professional integrity of their security forces. One might think enforcement would differentiate the army from other armies, contribute to added institutional identity in the purity of its violence and produce commensurate motivational gains for the agents.[44] So why, instead, do they try to make the issue go away?

6

Child abuse in the church and war crimes seem unrelated. After all, the church's control problems are unmitigated by the "fog of war," at least since the Crusades. For soldiers, conflict stress, confusion, and the heat of the action may result in hasty decisions with tragic consequences. These extenuating circumstances do not apply to atrocious behavior in the religious community. But neither are they a blanket cover for the army's failings. While some unlawful killings are accidental, the fog of war and these situational factors do not excuse the torture, humiliation, or killing of those in custody. Nor, presumably, can these fog of war factors excuse commanding officers, who stand by when their soldiers beat and kill innocent civilians, particularly with organizations that claim to value command responsibility, where a commander is responsible for subordinates'

---

[44] Berl Katznelson, a Jewish labor leader protesting the brutality of the conflict in British Mandate Palestine, advocated a "purity of arms" doctrine for the predecessor to the Israel Defence Force. See Tom Segev, *One Palestine Complete: Jews and Arabs Under the British Mandate*, trans. Hiam Watzman (New York: Metropolitan Books, 2000), p. 387.

wrongdoing, if she knew or should have known about it and did not take measures to prevent or punish it.

There is a common process underlying the relationship between leaders and followers in both types of organization, which is the negation of command responsibility. In the army and the church, the pattern of response to wrongdoing by those in charge is similar. Once the violation has occurred, those in the chain of command do not investigate, punish, or terminate those who commit sexual violence and knowingly break the Geneva Conventions. If they do anything, they assist the agent in keeping the shocking opportunism hidden. As far as one can tell from the evidence on career trajectories after providing this assistance, whether it is white-washing a terrible crime in Vietnam or moving a flock-abusing priest to new parishes, it does not appear to stand in the way of promotion. Grouping these crimes together reveals some common, salient, and theoretically interesting institutional characteristics and incentives at work that are highly relevant to understanding the puzzle of why principals— those higher in the chain of command—protect agents from the normal consequences of their opportunism.

In this setup, both clerical and war crimes are initiated by agents seeking a private benefit. The benefits are, no doubt, quite varied and obscure. It might be sex, sadism, revenge, bravado, peer approval, or the projection of feelings of vulnerability. The Black Watch soldiers in Iraq reportedly forced detainees to perform sexual acts on each other. One soldier said he had treated the fifty-two-year-old teacher "like his bitch."[45] In relation to sexual violence in the military and elsewhere, there is a long-running dispute about what exactly the agent is after—sex, power, or something else. Important progress has been made with this highly complex and difficult to research behavior to sort out types of sexual violence, the variety of motives, and the benefits conferred. Elisabeth Wood describes rape as a practice of war that is tolerated by commanders rather than adopted

---

[45] "Revealed: The Evidence of War Crimes Ministers Tried to Bury," *Sunday Times*, November 17, 2019. https://www.thetimes.co.uk/article/revealed-the-evidence-of-war-crimes-ministers-tried-to-bury-6x2fb63ts.

as a policy, and Dara Cohen's fieldwork provides insight: "Ex-combatants reported that those who participated in rape in Sierra Leone were seen to be more courageous, valiant, and brave than their peers . . . respected by their peers as "big men" . . . underscoring again that gang rape can be an effective method of increasing esteem and social ties between perpetrators."[46] As her work illustrates, the benefits plausibly include what individuals want for themselves and what they want from their peers and may impart some sense of cohesion.

The psychological processes for those perpetrating such serious offenses against another person are surely complex and heterogeneous. They are challenging to recover, from one individual's self-reports or confessions sometime after the event to the next. In fact, it may be so complex that the individual agents themselves do not know exactly what they were after in committing the crime, like the doctor with the "God complex." Getting a better grasp on an individual's impulses is important, yet for the logic of delegation some uncertainty is theoretically tolerable. Here, the important theoretical point is simply that there was some private gain sought under the auspices of performing their official duties. The agent used the authority granted not for God or for country. He used it for himself. Whatever the precise form the gratification took, be it sex, power, esteem, or acting out of revenge or contempt, or some potent emotion-fueled cocktail of all of these, he engaged in hidden action.[47] Why did he do so with impunity?

---

[46] Elisabeth Wood, "Armed Groups and Sexual Violence: When is Wartime Rape Rare," *Politics and Society* 37, no. 1 (2009): 131–162; Elisabeth Wood, "Rape as a Practice of War: Toward a Typology of Political Violence," *Politics and Society* 46, no. 4 (December 2018): 513–537; Dara Cohen, *Rape during Civil War* (Ithaca, NY: Cornell University Press 2016), 123. See also Gerald Schneider, Lilli Banholzer, and Laura Albarracin, "Ordered Rape: A Principal-Agent Analysis of Wartime Sexual Violence in the DR Congo," *Violence Against Women* 21 (2015): 1341–1363.

[47] For cross-national analyses of agent-centered violations such as torture and sexual violence see Christopher K. Butler, Tali Gluch and Neil J. Mitchell, "Security Forces and Sexual Violence: A Cross-National Analysis of a Principal—Agent Argument," *Journal of Peace Research*, 44, no. 6, (2007): 669–687; Alok K. Bohara, Neil J. Mitchell, Mani Nepal, and Nejem Raheem, "Human Rights Violations, Corruption, and the Policy of Repression," *The Policy Studies Journal*, 36, no. 1 (2008): 1–18.

7

The issue of selection is a good place to begin the analysis. The church and the army will attract a subset of unsuitable agents who present particular control problems. Armies are likely to attract some people who find particular gratification in violence. The Catholic Church likely attracts some people who find gratification in abuse. The combination of a church's access to children, a rule of celibacy that requires an unusual disposition on sexual relationships, and the exclusion of women from selection narrows a recruitment pool that is already contaminated by the tradition of abuse in the church, which provides a perverse apprenticeship for those entering the priesthood. The very high rates of abuse documented in Catholic residential institutions, where the Brethren are with the children around the clock, suggest that selection problems are pronounced in these institutions. In addition to attracting unfit agents, recruitment pressures and the difficulties of finding those willing to serve may dispose these organizations to accept riskier prospects. With the military, at times they may derive strategic benefits from selecting violent and abusive agents. But in the examples described here, there is little obvious organizational or strategic advantage from the killing of three Afghan sons that cost taxpayers an "assistance" payment, or abusing a teacher until he dies. The abuse is agent-centered, the gratification is private, and the collusion of those up the chain of command is retrospective.

After the event, neither the church nor the army took the expected measures to enforce formal punishment, regain control of their agents, and ensure future compliance with ethical and legal codes. In both organizations, the principal aids the agent in keeping the action hidden. Those in charge provide neither an honest account nor condign punishment. While the monitoring and punishment of agent opportunism is expected under principal-agent theory, unnoticed in the theory are the substantial costs to the principal, not just the agent, entailed in punishment and that are sufficient to dissuade a principal from administering it.

8

To develop a logic of delegation with wider application that goes "beyond the usual bounds of economic analysis," in Arrow's phrase, it is an important step to recognize that punishment is a more complex act than usually assumed. Punishing abuse is an option. But there are personal and governance incentives to be found in both organizations that work against its implementation. Personally, those in charge have the duty to manage their agents. Misconduct reflects a failure of leadership. We know the agent wants to keep the crime hidden. The Brother broke the child's arm for telling a doctor, or the soldier dropped a Russian pistol by the body. But also, up the chain of command, those in charge do not want to know of the crime. The atrocious event reflects on their competence to run the diocese or military unit. The exposure, if not the incidence of crimes, is a performance failure for those in charge. All the same, this motivation is likely to be quite general and not limited to managers in the types of organization under discussion.

In addition to the unremarkable, if not unimportant, personal incentive to cover up agent opportunism, there is a governance incentive at work. It has two components. Those in charge wish to protect the reputation of the organization. Again, there is nothing very novel in this claim. In the recent investigations of the Catholic Church, a central theme is of a hierarchy more concerned to protect the organization from reputational and serious financial damage, than to safeguard children. The exposure of abuse sends a negative signal about the institution to the congregation, or with the army, a negative signal to politicians controlling defense budgets and to the public.

But beyond burnishing the reputation of their organizations, I argue that principals seek to bolster the loyalty of their agents. For this reason, they have a strong incentive not to investigate and not to punish noncompliant agents. These incentives are most likely to be found where there is a single principal managing a group of specialized and cohesive agents. In this case it is not the act of abuse that binds these agents together, as Dara Cohen and Ragnhild Nordås find in their study of sexual violence among armed groups.[48] These agents cohere in resenting and resisting punishment to one of their number for the act of abuse. The threat or implementation of punishment sends a negative signal to the wider group of agents about the nature of the contract they have with the organization, and the anticipation of these agents acting together to raise the expected cost of punishment shifts the principal's incentives. Agents' willingness to cooperate to protect one of their number from punishment explains the lack of the expected and appropriate response from the principal. It explains the systematic, institution-wide, bottom-to-top cover-ups of clerical crimes and war crimes.

The principal needs to maintain the confidence of these agents and is concerned with balancing the demand for accountability from victims and external parties against the need to contain the impact of any punishment on the general loyalty, obedience, and effort supplied by the wider group of agents. Punishment, which is the principal's expected response to the untrustworthy agent, may send a negative signal to the entire group of agents. They may withdraw effort.

Principal-agent theorists recognize that monitoring and imposing punishment have some costs for the principal. It takes time and effort for the principal to monitor and impose punishment, and sometimes some agency losses are not worth the expense of correcting them. Some level of corruption may be tolerable for an organization. Yet, and beyond these costs, punishment can cause what it is usually thought to correct: noncompliance.

In some contexts, the narrowly self-interested agent assumption does not hold. Agents may possess an idea of professional responsibilities and learn to identify with the mission. The desire to serve God or country supplies intrinsically motivated agents. These agents find reward in delivering on the values imparted during the education process and training provided by the organization. But

[48] Dara Kay Cohen and Ragnhild Nordås, "Do States Delegate Shameful Violence to Militias? Patterns of Sexual Violence in Recent Armed Conflicts," *Journal of Conflict Resolution* 59, no. 1 (2015): 850–876.

the contents of a professional's values cannot be assumed. Along with religious and patriotic ideals, a more vital component of their esprit de corps is likely to be a strong sense of loyalty to each other. In this education process, they are likely to internalize and increasingly value the wellbeing of their comrades and fellows. Professional identity may refer to how agents identify with the organization's mission, ethics, and ideals and so has the benefit for the principal of reducing the need for monitoring and monetary incentives. But as Freud suggested when he examined the church and the army in *Group Psychology and the Analysis of the Ego*, the agents' identity also may be wrapped up with their fellow agents.[49] With these agents, their professionally fostered loyalty to each other encourages an "all for one and one for all" spirit. While this spirit is invaluable when confronting an enemy, when confronting a superior it can raise disciplinary issues. It disposes agents to rally around those in trouble. In ordering their preferences, these agents place the loyalty to each other over their loyalty to the mission. In punishing one, the principal may lose the confidence of the others.

In the standard models, it is the self-interested agent choosing the effort to give a task. In the identity economics and professional responsibilities models, it is "other-regarding" agents, or agents whose self-interest is filled with the mission of salvation and security, who choose the extra effort to give to a task. Here, it is agents whose self-interest is filled with feelings of loyalty to each other who decide whether or not to give effort to a task. The feelings of loyalty may be a complicated mix of love and fear; they love their brothers or sisters for the sacrifices they have made for each other, the dangers they have passed, and the rigorous discipline they have undergone; they fear being perceived as disloyal by the rest of the group, and the consequences that might follow from that. Again, without being able

---

[49] Sigmund Freud, *Group Psychology and the Analysis of the Ego* (London: W.W. Norton, [1921] 1975); Akerlof and Kranton (2010, p. 57), in their discussion of the role of identity, recognize the importance of workplace loyalties in the military. They provide an example of a crew covering up for a submarine commander. I explore the reverse scenario of crew member misconduct and the implications for the commander when confronted with wrong-doing in a "loyal workplace."

to pin down the precise psychological processes at work in the education of these agents and disentangling all the emotional threads that bind them together, the important theoretical point is that the identity of these agents is composed of a strong bond of loyalty to each other. As a consequence, "all for one" agents may be willing to withdraw effort not just on their own behalf, but on behalf of each other. It is this consideration that makes holding these agents to account so difficult and induces complicity by the principal.

The point might seem an obvious one with excessive punishment. Captain Bligh ran too tight a ship. There was a mutiny on the *Bounty*. Martinets with a cat o' nine tails sometimes achieve the opposite of the intended effect. But even appropriate punishment, if it is perceived to favor those who are outside the organization—for example, the victims—over those who are inside the organization, is a risky strategy for the principal. It may cause disillusionment or, in the extreme, mutiny in the ranks of these difficult-to-replace agents. In a reverse of the usual understanding of the relationship, loyalty demands flow both ways. Principals will be concerned to show their loyalty to their agents and to maintain agent confidence.

In short, what has been missed, even in a principal-agent theory informed by the recognition of the boost that professionalism and identity give to agents' efforts, is the difficulty the associated loyalties present in correcting opportunism among these agents when it does occur. Punishment of noncompliant agents is a more complex and more costly option for the principal where these loyalties are present and shape the cooperative preferences of groups of agents. The punishment of one underperforming agent may send a signal to fellow agents to withdraw their effort. Principals must maintain the confidence of their agents, as well as the other way around; they must attend to the *agent confidence factor*. A "band of brothers" is clearly desirable in a military unit. The trouble is that under some conditions, the brothers may value their brotherhood and obligation to a fellow professional over their responsibility to the profession. The bonds created among these agents, their willingness to hang together rather than separately if you like, and as a consequence the extra costs that punishing them impose on the principal, present a substantial obstacle to successful delegation. The severe control problems in the army and the Catholic Church illustrate the importance of this modification to the standard account of a singular, self-interested agent.

9

The violence and abuse under discussion are very grave. From outside these organizations it may seem surprising that agents would value their loyalty to each other more highly than responding to shameful abuse. Ideally, they should welcome punishment as a sign of the integrity of the institution and as consistent with their professional identity. Instead, the harm done the victim is depreciated. Perversely, attention switches to the struggle and suffering of the perpetrator. The perpetrators, priests and soldiers, are depicted as unlike ordinary people. They have endured privation in following a higher, sacred, or heroic purpose, suggesting that ordinary standards of behavior should not apply when these individuals "lapse." The response within these organizations is to rationalize misconduct by fellow agents, resort to euphemism, use epithets to dehumanize the victims, and keep the agents' actions hidden.

The Australian inquiry into the church points to this type of response: "The failure to understand that the sexual abuse of a child was a crime with profound impacts for the victim, and not a mere moral failure capable of correction by contrition and penance (a view expressed in the past by a number of religious leaders) is almost incomprehensible."[50] The difficulty of maintaining celibacy led to abuse being viewed as "forgivable moral lapses committed by colleagues who were struggling to live up to an ideal." Confession "enabled perpetrators to resolve their sense of guilt without fear of being reported."[51] Confession provided a low-cost emotional release for the perpetrators and no safety for the victim. One

---

[50] Royal Commission (2017), p. 8.
[51] Ibid., pp. 71, 73.

young girl divulged in confession what another priest was doing to her. She was told that she was a "disgusting girl" and given ten Hail Marys and ten Our Fathers. A priest confessed to raping at least fifteen boys aged seven and up. He was complimented on his "candor and sincerity" and for the "progress he has made" with his "addiction."[52] Penance and prayer ensured against accountability in this world.

For the army, the "fog of war" and the heat of the action explain some of what happens. But the killing and rape at My Lai happened without an enemy present. One soldier testified that "the boys enjoyed it" . . . more than forty participated in the killing, and "not a single soldier on the ground tried to stop the killing. Nor did anyone try to stop the rapes."[53] A helicopter crew did intervene to protect some of the villagers. The Royal Marine who killed the Taliban described his action accurately as breaking the Geneva Convention. He rationally warned his fellow marines to keep quiet about what he had done, yet his action was seen as a lapse for he was released on grounds of diminished responsibility.

To be clear, I am not arguing that all armies are the same in how they handle the stress of conflict, in depicting and dehumanizing the enemy and in committing these types of violations. Depending on the leadership available, their ideological commitment, and the discipline imposed, there are vast differences between armies in the restraint they exercise in dealing with civilian populations and noncombatants and in terms of the scale of violations committed.[54] Those armies with leaders that have paid attention to recruitment and selection issues and in inculcating the importance of rules of conduct make a difference. But when violations are committed, the response of those in command is normally determined by the agent confidence factor, rather than maintaining the integrity of the institution. Of course, it is a choice, and a few leaders do rise to the occasion.

[52] 40th Statewide Investigating Grand Jury, Report 1 (2018), p. 4.
[53] Howard Jones, *My Lai: Vietnam, 1968, and the Descent into Darkness* (New York: Oxford University Press, 2017), pp. 107, 349.
[54] See Neil J. Mitchell, *Agents of Atrocity* (New York: Palgrave Macmillan, 2004).

Shakespeare's Henry V is one. After the siege of Harfleur in 1415, Henry's army is en route to Agincourt. Bardolph, a soldier, steals an object from a French church. He is to be hanged for this crime. Group loyalty and the agent confidence factor intervene in the form of Ancient Pistol, a fellow soldier and "sworn brother" of Bardolph. He pleads vehemently on Bardolph's behalf to prevent the punishment. The king, notified of the pending execution, is told the name of the perpetrator. Bardolph was one of Henry's drinking companions when he was fun-loving Prince Hal. But as king, Henry is aware of his responsibilities. He supports the chain of command, saying, "We would have all such offenders so cut off, and we here give express charge that in our marches through the country there be nothing compelled from the villages, nothing taken but paid for, none of the French upbraided or abused in disdainful language [no war on "cunts" and "bitches"]. For when lenity and cruelty play for a kingdom, the gentler gamester is the soonest winner."[55] Here is an early statement of the importance of winning hearts and minds, valuing outsiders over insiders, and in this case of resisting the pressure of group loyalties in the name of the mission. Here is a leader able to distance himself from former cronies, able to maintain discipline, and famously then able to call to arms "we happy few, we band of brothers." Henry's pep talk before Agincourt is surely familiar in military academies such as Westpoint or Sandhurst, but the treatment of Bardolph is a relevant teaching point as well.

Loyalty is a defining feature of organizations like the church and the army. These agents are a chosen few. Clerics live their lives in a religious community. It is a commonplace that soldiers fight for each other as much as, if not more than, for an ideology or a country.[56] They share their working and nonworking lives together in these organizations. While a military career is not for life, veterans' associations preserve the bonds forged in military service long after individuals leave. Principals are aware of these bonds and the need to maintain agent confidence. It is not that the army, for example,

---

[55] *Henry V*, Act III, Scene 6.
[56] See, for example, Dora Costa and Matthew Kahn, *Heroes and Cowards: The Social Face of War* (Princeton, NJ: Princeton University Press, 2008).

never imposes disciplinary measures. Discipline, formal and informal, may be fierce.[57] But it is so normally for those who betray the group. If an individual soldier acts opportunistically and decides on flight rather than fight and endangers his or her brothers and sisters, then the punishment consequences are severe. With war crimes, on the other hand, punishment is generally not fitted to the crime. Punishment, or the lack of it, is fitted to group loyalty, the signal it sends to the rest of the group, and the need to maintain agent confidence. Given the strength of these group attachments, disciplining, dismissing, or convicting a brother or a comrade for what they have done to those outside the group may affect the willingness of others within the group to continue to serve. Disillusioned, they may withdraw their effort.

The difficulty of replacing agents reinforces the salience of the agent confidence factor and works to decrease or tokenize the punishment administered. Asset specificity is the tailoring of an asset for a particular purpose. High specificity means it lacks other uses. A blend of nature and training gives these agents high asset specificity. Service in the church or the military requires a substantial investment in specialized training. Most notably for the church, there are limited if any other uses for this training. To get individuals to make this investment, those in charge of these organizations need to be able to offer something in exchange. The range of incentives available is constrained by the characteristics of an organization. Money is a powerful incentive, but getting rich in military or religious service seems contrary to the ethos. High salaries are unseemly for organizations passing collection bowls or dependent on taxpayers. Beyond God and country, what has the principal to offer?

If individuals joins an organization that prepares them for little else, then they will want a secure contract. Economists Eugene Fama and Michael Jensen, in their examination of the survival of organizations characterized by the separation of ownership and control, include nonprofits such as the Catholic Church, where donors do not

[57] For a discussion of the role of punishment, see Peter Feaver, *Armed Servants: Agency, Oversight, and Civil Military Relations* (Cambridge, MA: Harvard University Press, 2003).

make the important decisions. They suggest that the strength of the bond of priests to the church helps explain organizational survival in this case. They remark on the asset specificity of the Catholic priest-hood, for which they receive security of contract. The priest "cannot offer his services on a competitive basis. In exchange for developing such organization-specific human capital, the Catholic priest, unlike his Protestant and Jewish counterparts, gets a lifetime contract that promises a real standard of living."[58] These scholars argue that the contract keeps the agents' interests aligned with their "donor-customers." In contrast to this view, I argue that maintaining the security of contract is precisely the problem for the congregation. When priests abuse, their contracts remain secure. The priority that those in charge place on retaining rather than dismissing the agent creates collusion in keeping hidden actions hidden, at the expense of the donors and congregations.

The agents are asked to reshape their lives, undergo specialized and lengthy training, and perform difficult service. In return, they expect job security. This reciprocity reinforces the reluctance to punish. If you ask agents to do the difficult service, they will likely see that it is only fair that you then have to back them. With the army, former British Defence Secretary Gavin Williamson says of the British soldiers who had escaped formal punishment for almost fifty years for the 1972 Bloody Sunday killing of thirteen unarmed civil rights marchers in Northern Ireland: "Bloody Sunday prosecutions would turn the stomachs of the British people" and the British government "had to do something to make sure our soldiers and veterans have the protection they deserve."[59] The morale of agents and their willingness to expend effort for the principal are likely to be affected not only by the incentives offered and the intrinsic rewards of living up to their ideals, but by the losses and punishments they and their fellow agents receive within the organization. Those in charge have to manage *the agent confidence factor.*

---

[58] Eugene Fama and Michael C. Jensen, "The Separation of Ownership and Control," *The Journal of Law and Economics* 26, no. 2 (June 1983): 320.

[59] "Minister Seeks 10-year Limit on Prosecutions of Soldiers," *Sunday Times*, March 3, 2019. https://www.thetimes.co.uk/article/minister-seeks-10-year-limit-on-prosecutions-of-soldiers-sctcrrhgj. The Northern Ireland minister at the time, Karen Bradley, even went so far as to deny that the soldiers had committed any crimes.

The army and the church face difficulties replacing their agents in the short term. They will be reluctant to impose termination or disciplinary measures on individual members for fear of the signal it sends to the wider group, who may reduce or withdraw their effort. Given the recruitment challenges for these organizations, the need for a highly motivated workforce, and the leverage this gives agents, principals choose not to investigate and punish opportunism, as punishment can create, not just correct, noncompliance.

10

When misconduct occurs, both the church and the army rely on agent confessions and self-reports and leave it to bishops and commanders to manage the investigation. The bishop handles allegations of abuse for the diocese and relies on the perpetrator's admission of "sin." The bishop files complaints in his secret archive. If the abuse is exposed, the perpetrator is sent to a church treatment center, or transferred to a "benevolent bishop" in another diocese. According to the Pennsylvania Grand Jury, the police are not informed and the offending priest is put on "sick leave," or is described as recovering from "nervous exhaustion."

In the United States Army, commanders manage wrongdoing by those under their commands and rely heavily on self-reporting, as the Amnesty International 2014 report "Left in the Dark" makes clear: "Most importantly, the military justice system is 'commander-driven' and, to a large extent, relies on soldiers' own accounts of their actions in assessing the legality of a given operation . . . the functioning of the system depends very much on initial, ground-level reporting from troops at the point of contact. It is, in significant ways, a system of self-policing."[60] On his 2009 visit to the United States, the UN Special Rapporteur on Summary and Extrajudicial Executions came to a similar conclusion about the

---

[60] Amnesty International (2014), p. 2.

commander-driven system, the lack of transparency, the failure to investigate and the inappropriate sentences.

Covering up does not appear to harm a military career, any more than it does a church career. Max Hastings describes a memorandum from 23rd Division staff officer Major Colin Powell, concerning war crimes in Vietnam, as an "uncompromising whitewash."[61] Major Powell later became Chairman of the Joint Chiefs of Staff, National Security Advisor, and Secretary of State. In the chain of delegation, bishops and commanders have it within their power to manage investigations and help hide agent misconduct. It is not clear that promotion is a reward for covering up, but those who tolerate and conceal agent opportunism in order to maintain agent loyalty do so without obvious adverse consequences for their careers in the organization. Covering up has not prevented entry to the College of Cardinals, nor to the top jobs in the military.

11

Those in the chain of command are not holding subordinates to account. But what other evidence is there for the agent confidence factor, aside from the failure to live up to the responsibility of command? The key dimension of the agent confidence factor is the group's loyalty to the abuser. It is this loyalty that provides a strong incentive for the commander not to investigate and not to punish for fear that others will withdraw their effort. Without this loyalty, the cost of punishment would be much lower for the principal and, indeed, the task of gathering evidence against the abuser would be substantially easier.

An indicator of group loyalty is the success of these agents in overcoming the temptation to inform on each other if they are under investigation. The British Army's Aitken Report in 2008 described some cases of the unlawful killing and abuse of Iraqi civilians, not

---

[61] Hastings (2018), p. 21.

done in the heat of the moment or when the soldiers feared for their lives. The report finds that prisoners do not "defect," as in the proverbial prisoner's dilemma, and that court-martial judges encountered a "wall of silence." The report describes the challenge the army faces "to educate our people to understand that lying to the Service Police, or having 'selective memory loss' in court, in order to protect other members of their unit, are not forms of loyalty, but rather a lack of integrity."[62] If misconduct gets as far as a court-martial, this report specifically identifies the loyalty agents have to each other as the key explanation for the unwillingness of these agents to inform on their fellow agents who are charged with war crimes.

Loyalty may be driven by fear to discourage defection. The *Vanity Fair* journalist William Langewiesche describes the courage of an individual soldier to break silence on a war crime and the complicity of commanders who do not want to know. He points out that war crimes are substantially underreported because of the risks a "snitch" assumes. In the example he describes, revenge was how American soldiers characterized their motive for the killing of some Iraqi detainees, although there seems a "big man" dynamic at work as well:

" 'Hey, what we did was for Soto and Guerrero. . . . It stays in this group, this brotherhood. . . . And don't worry. If anything ever comes up, it'll start with me and end with me. I'll fall on the sword.' "[63] The whistle-blower, Cunningham, helped to convict the perpetrators, but only once he had left Iraq. In Iraq, he feared the informal enforcement measures other members of the "brotherhood" might take to protect the group *at the expense* of their professional responsibilities.

The My Lai case is a usefully hard test for the agent confidence factor. The scale and gravity of the war crime, with murder, gang rape and sexual violence, and victims in the hundreds would seem

---

[62] *The Aitken Report: An Investigation into Cases of Deliberate Abuse and Unlawful Killing in Iraq in 2003 and 2004*, The British Army (January 25, 2008), p. 24. http://image.guardian. co.uk/sys-files/Guardian/documents/2008/01/25/aitken_rep.pdf.

[63] William Langewiesche, "How One U.S. Soldier Blew the Whistle on a Cold-Blooded War Crime," *Vanity Fair*, June 16, 2015 https://www.vanityfair.com/news/2015/06/iraq-war-crime-army-cunningham-hatley-trial.

to make a failure to deliver appropriate punishment incomprehensible, even to fellow soldiers. Many victims were women and children. If we find evidence for loyalty to the perpetrators in an atrocity of this scale and nastiness among other soldiers who were not perpetrators, then we are likely to find it more generally. There is evidence of this loyalty. When Lieutenant Calley was convicted for the massacre, Calley had the support of other American soldiers far beyond his unit: "War correspondents in Vietnam saw numerous indications of troop support for Calley, including an artillery piece painted with the words 'Calley's Revenge' and a sign declaring, 'Kill a gook for Calley.'"[64] Serving soldiers supported him, as did those in charge of recruiting soldiers, and recruits themselves.

There was an immediate and very negative reaction to Calley's punishment in the United States from recruits and those drafting soldiers to serve in Vietnam. At Fort Benning, recruits sang "Calley . . . Calley . . . He's our man" and a local Alabama group had a hit (200,000 records sold) with a pro-Calley number.[65] The agent confidence mechanism requires reciprocity for the sacrifices the agent has made on the organization's behalf. It requires those in command to bolster loyalty and ignore "unfair" calls for accountability and punishment. The reaction of those on the draft boards included withdrawing their effort, resigning from the draft boards in ten or more states, threatening not to induct anyone, and otherwise indicating their disillusionment with the punishment of Calley: "A board in Kentucky unanimously agreed that Calley had been 'unjustly persecuted'. . . . Board members sought assurances from the administration against future draftees undergoing the same treatment."[66] This reaction is strong evidence of the expectation that leaders "back their men," of security of contract, and of the agent confidence factor.

---

[64] Jones (2017), 304.
[65] Max Hastings, *Vietnam: An Epic Tragedy, 1945-1974* (London: William Collins, 2018), p. 544.
[66] Jones (2017), 299.

Calley's case was unusual in that he was convicted. In the brutal Kenya counterinsurgency that Britain fought in the 1950s, the historian Huw Bennett describes a very difficult choice facing the general in command. General Erskine had to choose between "impartial military justice or damaged military morale, threatening his ability to conduct the campaign." He chose to preserve morale and "numerous military crimes against civilians went unpunished. . . . By protecting those involved in the Chuka massacre, Sergeant Allen and his askaris, and those accused of rape, murder, beatings and torture at the McLean Inquiry and elsewhere, General Erskine prevented a mutiny in the security forces."[67] In *The History Thieves*, Ian Cobain tells the fascinating story of the lengths the British government went to in order to hide information about how this war was fought and the wrongdoing of its agents.[68] Accountability finally came in court in 2011. The British government refused formally to admit liability, but did agree to make compensation payments to the survivors of torture inflicted by its forces in the 1950s.

For historians, the choice to protect the agents from the consequences of their actions may seem more obvious than it does to the social scientist. Indeed, Edward Gibbon describes the flexible management practices of Roman emperors, concerned about the contract they had with their elite but temperamental Praetorian guards. To maintain the confidence of "such formidable servants" they had "to mix blandishments with commands, rewards with punishments, flatter their pride, indulge their pleasures, connive at their irregularities and purchase their precarious faith by a liberal donative."[69] The philosopher David Hume uses a similar example, pointing to the precariousness of command: "The soldan of Egypt

[67] Huw Bennett, *Fighting the Mau Mau* (Cambridge: Cambridge University Press, 2012), p. 218.

[68] For a detailed account of how the British government destroyed and hid its records see Ian Cobain, *The History Thieves: Secret, Lies and the Shaping of a Modern Nation* (London: Portobello Books, 2016); see also David Anderson, *Histories of the Hanged: The Dirty War in Kenya and the End of Empire* (London: W. W. Norton. 2005).

[69] Edward Gibbon, *The History of the Decline and Fall of the Roman Empire*, I (London: The Folio Society, 1983), p. 114.

or the emperor of Rome might drive his harmless subjects like brute beasts. . . . But he must, at least, have led his mamalukes or praetorian bands, like men, by their opinion."[70]

For the principal-agent theorist, General Erskine's choice is surprising, shows that the conventional theory needs modification, and clearly illustrates the importance of considering the context of multiple agents, the organizational culture and bonds they develop, and the agent confidence factor as an explanation of the passivity of the principal. Units vary in the intensity of group loyalties. The entry requirements, level of training, and degree of trust among members of the Special Forces and elite regiments, Roman and otherwise, make these units efficient. These agents are part of a group where narrow self-interest is *not* the expected norm. By joining these forces, they show a yet higher level of idealism and commitment to their country and presumably to each other. In addition, the screening and training of these agents make them hard to replace. Factors that make for efficiency, also in the event of misconduct, make these agents the most difficult to hold to account and control. In 2004 in Iraq, a British Special Forces soldier shot and killed an Iraqi civilian, Ghanin Gatteh al-Roomi. The SAS soldier was the first serving soldier in the history of his regiment to be charged with murder. His immediate commanders opposed charging the soldier. Posing General Erskine's choice and illustrating the agent confidence factor, his comrades threatened to resign if the matter was pursued. A senior officer stated: "this is one of the worst crises the SAS has ever faced . . . the commanding officer has been told by many of his troops that if the soldier is found guilty of murder they will terminate their SAS careers. They can't believe that the Army chiefs have allowed this to happen."[71] The charges were dropped.

Finally, to return to the Royal Marine who killed the Taliban, fellow soldiers had to be dissuaded from attending a public demonstration

---

[70] David Hume, "Of the First Principles of Government," in *Hume's Moral and Political Philosophy*, ed. Henry D. Aiken (New York: Hafner Press, 1948), p. 307.

[71] "Soldiers Will Quit SAS over Trooper on Murder Charge," *The Telegraph*, March 6, 2005. https://www.telegraph.co.uk/news/uknews/1485038/Soldiers-will-quit-SAS-over-trooper-on-murder-charge.html.

in London in support of the marine: "Fearing a public show of support from troops" commanders "have repeatedly warned them they face disciplinary punishment if they attend." Agent loyalties even extended to United States Marines, some of whom were expected at the demonstration. One of the organizers of the rally stated that "there is a lot of support coming through from serving personnel who have confirmed that the MoD [Ministry of Defence] has issued orders that they are not to attend a political protest, however this is not a political protest it is a show of support to one of our fellow Royal Marines."[72] The fine balance in managing agent loyalty, so valuable in war and so harmful in maintaining the laws of war, requires much of those in command. In both American and British war crimes, from Kenya and Vietnam to Iraq and Afghanistan, there is evidence of the mutual bonds of agent loyalty extending to those who violate the laws of war and the generation of a powerful pressure on commanders not to punish. Shakespeare's Henry V aside, commanders generally bow to this pressure.

Disloyalty to abusive agents in the church is also rare. One notable whistle-blower, Richard Sipe, left the priesthood in 1970. Disturbed by what he had seen in the church, he interviewed perpetrators and victims. His work encouraged investigative journalists at the *Boston Globe*, portrayed in the movie *Spotlight*. He connected the abuse to church practices and to celibacy. Sipe estimated that only 50 percent of priests were celibate: "when men in authority—cardinals, bishops rectors, abbots, confessors, professors—are having or have had an unacknowledged-secret-active sex life under the guise of celibacy, an atmosphere of tolerance of behaviors within the system is made operative."[73] In *Sex, Priests, and Secret Codes: The Catholic Church's 2,000 Year Paper Trail of Sexual Abuse*,[74] Sipe and coauthors describe

[72] "Troops Warned Not to Attend Sgt. Alexander Blackman Rally," *Daily Telegraph*, October 26, 2015. https://www.telegraph.co.uk/news/uknews/defence/11956351/Troops-warned-not-to-attend-Sgt-Alexander-Blackman-rally.html.
[73] "A. W. Richard Sipe, a Leading Expert on Clergy Sex Abuse, Dies at 85," *New York Times*, August 9, 2018. https://www.nytimes.com/2018/08/09/nyregion/aw-richard-sipe-a-leading-voice-on-clergy-sex-abuse-dies-at-85.html.
[74] A. W. Richard Sipe, Thomas Doyle, and Patrick J. Wall, *Sex, Priests, and Secret Codes: The Catholic Church's 2,000 Year Paper Trail of Sexual Abuse* (London: Crux, 2016).

the strength of the clerical brotherhood, the premium on keeping its secrets, and the courage required of any priest to reveal the sex crimes of his peers. Decision-makers in the church preferred to keep the actions of their agents hidden and to protect their security of employment, rather than expose and punish.

Both the organizations' standard operating procedures and their claims of higher purpose help confound effective monitoring and third-party oversight. Both organizations have their own legal systems, without effective external checks. Civilian authorities generally do not interfere. An Irish policeman said his superiors did not want to know about clerical abuse: "They washed their hands of it," he said. The victims, he added, "were dismissed as if they didn't matter. The power of the clergy was so strong."[75] It took the media and third-party victims' rights groups, like Broken Rites Australia, to sound the alarm.

12

In contrast to the church, the chain of delegation for Western militaries stretches back to civilian authorities, who themselves are responsible to the electorate. This ultimate principal is ideally a repository of rule-of-law values. But here again the incentives do not work as expected in theory. The electorate lets theorists down.

To survive politically, democratic leaders are expected to deliver public goods, including human rights. These leaders are accountable periodically to ordinary citizens: "accountability appears to be the critical feature that makes full-fledged democracies respect human rights."[76] But when it comes to their troops' war crimes, presidents and prime ministers in full-fledged democracies do not deliver accountability.

[75] "As Pope Visits Ireland Scars of Sex Abuse Worse than the IRA," *New York Times*, August 23, 2018. https://www.nytimes.com/2018/08/23/world/europe/francis-ireland-sexual-abuse-catholic-church.html.

[76] Bruce Bueno de Mesquita, George W. Downs, Alastair Smith, and Feryal Marie Cherif, "Thinking Inside the Box: A Closer Look at Democracy and Human Rights," *International Studies Quarterly* 49, no. 3 (2005): 439.

Politicians must be seen to be loyal to the troops, whom they have placed in the difficult conflict situations in the first place. They are concerned about maintaining the confidence of their agents, on the one side, and on the other, the reaction of the ultimate principal, the voters. But these pressures are reinforcing, not countervailing. Allegations of war crimes are seen as unfair by the soldiers and unpatriotic by the voters, as John Kerry found out to his cost in his 2004 presidential campaign. On his visit to the United States, the UN Special Rapporteur described war crimes prosecutions as "politically radioactive."[77] Other democracies treat them as similarly hazardous. The Israeli soldier Elor Azaria shot and killed a prone and wounded Palestinian in March 2016 in Hebron. The killing was on video. Azaria received an eighteen-month sentence for manslaughter. He served nine months. Prime Minister Benjamin Netanyahu called for a pardon. Democratic political leaders do not want to punish these agents for wrongdoing. Significantly, Israeli President Reuven Rivlin refused a pardon, though at the cost of being branded a traitor by some.[78] On his release, Azaria reportedly was greeted as a hero.

Politicians need to maintain the loyalty of their security services and answer to voters. Despite expectations that this final link in the chain of delegation would reconnect political leaders with the rule of law, the public does not care to make this connection and provide a check on elected officials. The evidence from My Lai and elsewhere suggests the public does not compensate for political and military leaders' failure to investigate and to punish war crimes. It reinforces the incentive to make war crimes go away. It offers no effective check on institutionalized coverups. The public supports their troops, irregularities and all. With clear evidence of dreadful wrongdoing, as at My Lai, the majority of the American public took the perpetrator's

---

[77] United Nations General Assembly, *Report of the Special Rapporteur on Extrajudicial, Summary or Arbitrary Executions* (May 28, 2009), p. 28.
[78] "Elor Azaria, Israeli Soldier Convicted of Killing a Wounded Palestinian Terrorist Set Free after Nine Months," *Haaretz*, May 8, 2018. https://www.haaretz.com/israel-news/ .premium-hebron-shooter-elor-azaria-released-from-prison-after-nine-months-1.6070371.

side. Secretary of Defense Melvin Laird observed that "public opinion rallied around the soldiers accused in the massacre."[79] In the case of the Royal Marine who broke the Geneva Convention and shot the wounded Taliban, public demonstrations were in support of the marine, not the law. According to one national newspaper, the British "public demands leniency for Royal Marine who murdered Taliban fighter."[80] The British Operation Northmoor investigation into war crimes in Afghanistan by Special Forces troops was made to "go away," according to a "well-placed government source," because it was seen as a "potential disaster for the government." What the government is "desperately trying to do is trying to avoid any detail of the accusations getting into the press and thereby undermining, in their view, national security, public trust [and] work with allies."[81] The Operation was initiated as a result of complaints about civilian deaths from another soldier (who was not Special Forces) and from the Red Cross. To raise questions about the abuse and killing of civilians led to questions about one's patriotism, according to one commentator.[82] Democratic governments that place troops in difficult places must be seen to support their troops. In this climate of opinion, opposition political parties have nothing to gain in campaigning on this issue and holding the government to account.

To return to John Stuart Mill, he anticipated this failing and the key role of the voting public in the accountability process: "if the public, the mainspring of the whole checking machinery, are too ignorant, too passive, or too careless and inattentive to do their part, little benefit will be derived from the best administrative apparatus. . . . if the

---

[79] Melvin Laird, *With Honor* (Madison: University of Wisconsin Press, 2008), p. 100.

[80] "Public Demands Leniency for Royal Marine Who Murdered Taliban Fighter," *Mail Online*, December 7, 2013. https://www.dailymail.co.uk/news/article-2520053/Public-demands-Royal-Marine-murdered-Taliban-fighter-sentence-halved.html. See Herbert C. Kelman and V. Lee Hamilton, *Crimes of Obedience: Toward a Social Psychology of Authority and Responsibility* (New Haven, CT: Yale University Press, 1989).

[81] "Revealed: How the Inquiry Was 'Made to Go Away,'" *Sunday Times*, July 2, 2017. https://www.thetimes.co.uk/article/revealed-how-inquiry-into-sas-unit-accused-of-executing-civilians-was-made-to-go-away-investigation-kill-killing-mod-ministry-defence-xt0mszl0k.

[82] "Why We May Never Know if British Troops Committed War Crimes in Iraq," *The Guardian*, June 7, 2018. https://www.theguardian.com/news/2018/jun/07/british-troops-war-crimes-iraq-historic-allegations-team?CMP=share_btn_link.

public will not look at what is done."[83] Whether in presidential or parliamentary systems, the integrity of an accountability mechanism relies on the public, and in general, they will not look at what is done. While bishops and those above them in the chain of delegation knowingly protect opportunistic agents, the pressures on the church are different. The Pope is not appointed by the congregation. Nevertheless, he is reportedly becoming concerned about the impact of abuse, made visible by external inquiries, on that congregation. Ironically, the chance of reform as a result of pressure from below in this non-democratic organization appears greater than the chance of the public getting out of the habit of going along with war crimes. The victims are from within the flock, and they may be motivated to show their dismay. While the congregation does not control leader selection, attendance and donations matter to the survival of the organization. The Pope is unelected but is not unaffected by sanction from the congregation. The gathering public evidence and outrage in the congregation may constrain the leadership's complicity with the abusers, indicate to other agents that there are limits to loyalty, and help to cure the civilian authorities of their neglect of the victims and their habitual deference to the church.

13

In relying on agents with specialized skills and knowledge and who are difficult to replace, the principal has a problem. Professional responsibility and an esprit de corps are essential to the functioning of organizations, as Kenneth Arrow recognized. But the formal enforcement of professional ethics is not as available as he suggested. When a professional goes rogue, fellow agents may herd around. It takes an exceptional leader to confront such a problem, as Shakespeare recognized in setting this very leadership test for his Henry V. Punishment entails costs for the principal as well as the

---

[83] John Stuart Mill, *Considerations on Representative Government* (Rockville, MD: Serenity Press, [1861] 2008), p. 27.

agent and, in contrast to the familiar depiction of the principal-agent relationship, principals need to maintain the confidence of agents.

In describing some of this work to an academic colleague, he asked why I focused on Western militaries. He pointed out that the armies of dictators are far worse. True enough, but democracies claim to be different. A central claim made for democracies by academics and democratic leaders alike is the role of accountability. But when it comes to abuses, neither democratic theory nor principal-agent theory provides a good guide to how those in charge behave.

I have used real-world examples to illustrate the causal processes and to give some prima facie plausibility to the argument, which is open to empirical challenge. Those who commit these crimes at little cost to themselves belong to secretive, hierarchical organizations that claim a higher purpose and, importantly, place a high priority on internal group loyalty. Wherever we find war crimes, for example, we should find a reluctance to investigate and to punish, in France or Canada as well as the United Kingdom and the United States. Agents within these organizations will be unwilling to inform on each other. If crimes are exposed by investigative reporters, as at My Lai, then the expectation is that the punishment will be substantially lighter than for a comparable crime in civilian life, and punishment will be less likely as one moves up the chain of delegation. The military doctrine of command responsibility will be more honored in the breach, in the ordinary sense of that phrase. The expectation is that commanders will not respond appropriately to their subordinates' abuses. Instead, they will aid agents in keeping their actions hidden. Where loyalties are most intense and training most specialized, for example in elite regiments such as the British Parachute Regiment, the United States Marines and Special Forces, investigation and punishment of war crimes is least likely: the more specialized and difficult to replace the asset, the less likely is punishment.

For their part, the expectation is that civilian political leaders will not want to know and will not seek accountability when their own troops commit crimes. I stated that from Richard Nixon to Boris Johnson, political leaders have sought to avoid rather than assist accountability, but the same should hold for the presidents and prime ministers in between. And the electorate's commitment to human rights will be conditioned by the nationality of the perpetrator. Political leaders act on the highly plausible proposition that the public will not have a "stomach" for prosecuting their own soldiers. Survey research can open this proposition to empirical test.[84] Finally, while the church and the military are special, other organizations, the police for example, and professions, including the medical profession, that develop human asset specificity and difficult-to-replace agents, that foster strong bonds among agents and whose service is wrapped in a higher purpose (God, country, the Hippocratic Oath), are likely to display at least a measure of paradoxical incapacity to discipline rogue members.

If we take reducing sex crimes and war crimes by these agents as desirable, rather than the narrower goals of those presently in charge in the hierarchies, we need to get closer to Arrow's understanding of professionalism as "systems of ethics, internalized during the education process and enforced in some measure by formal punishments and more broadly by reputations." Given that those within the chain of delegation cannot be trusted, more outside controls on the operation of the organizations are required. Reliance on civilian authorities by the military may be less straightforward. But with the pressure exerted by the agent confidence factor, the investigation and prosecution of these crimes should be a discrete task, less dependent on the commander's discretion. The unreliability of civilian politicians and the electorate where their own soldiers are concerned, supports the case for a last resort to international authorities (as provided in the Rome Statute of the International Criminal Court) with no conflicting incentives.

In reshaping this element of the burden of command, reform might even be welcomed by those under pressure from below and above. The legal doctrine of "command responsibility" is designed to encourage military officers to take control of their subordinates, but it needs reinforcement. While the former head of the British

---

[84] Dr. Niheer Dasandi (University of Birmingham) and I have designed a survey experiment to test this link in the causal argument.

army, General Sir Mike Jackson, told the inquiry into the killing
in British custody of Iraqi hotel receptionist Baha Mousa that "it
is absolutely bedrock to the British Army's philosophy that a commanding officer is responsible for what goes on within his command," instances of its operation are very hard to find—another
empirical challenge. For example, on Bloody Sunday, Jackson was
on the scene as a captain in the Parachute Regiment. According
to information collected by the Saville Inquiry into that event, it
was a breach of discipline by the soldiers. It was a principal-agent
problem. But immediately after the unlawful killing, Jackson
helped prepare an inaccurate account that stated that the victims
were armed. He denied participating in a cover-up.[85] No officer
took any responsibility at the time for what were later found to be
unlawful killings and the alleged ill-discipline of the elite regiment.
As noted, Jackson went on to the top job. Longer term, selecting
agents carefully, re-examining factors that limit the recruitment
pool, and creating, as the British Army Aitken report suggested,
a professional esprit de corps that values virtuous conduct and
loyalty to a law-abiding institution with a long and honorable tradition over loyalty to rogue members of the profession are likely
the most powerful mechanisms in restraining agent opportunism,
yet also the most difficult to implement.

[85] Richard Norton-Taylor, "Army Chief Questioned over 'Shot List,'" *The Guardian*, October
16, 2003. https://www.theguardian.com/uk/2003/oct/16/bloodysunday.northernireland.

4
Agreement

If not to happiness, there is a route through delegation to resolving disagreement. Delegating to a dispute-resolving agent prevents social and economic life from grinding to a halt. Parties to a marriage contract or a trade treaty fall out from time to time. A way forward is to find an autonomous agent to council, mediate, or decide the matter. It is a division of labor that facilitates economic progress, as does delegating tasks on the production line. Without the expectation of some method of adjudicating disputes and getting both sides to live up to agreements, we would be reluctant to invest our energy and time in an enterprise. Ordinary life would become intolerable. Even a game of football would be problematic. To get things underway, players agree to the rules of the game and to the idea of a neutral referee with the discretion to interpret and enforce the rules. Once underway, the players, partial to their own interests, do what they can to fool or bias the referee.

For joint endeavors and the games we play, we need rules, confidence that they will be interpreted fairly, and some capacity to be a good loser in this type of delegation relationship. Not all the agent's decisions will be favorable, all of the time. Some scholars argue that with his unusual autonomy and the latitude to make decisions at the expense of the principal, this agent escapes the theory. They use the term *trustee* instead. But following Occam's razor, terms should not be added unnecessarily. As David Lake and Matthew McCubbins say, incomplete control is central to principal-agent theory, and "trusteeship status" is "fully expected by the theory and follows from the need for substantial autonomy to perform the tasks for which

Why Delegate?. Neil J. Mitchell, Oxford University Press (2021). © Oxford University Press.
DOI: 10.1093/oso/9780190904197.003.0004

courts are responsible."[1] The dispute-resolver is consistent with the simpler theory, with the mechanisms it describes and the struggle for control that it depicts. This delegation is set up under the norm of impartiality in order to induce parties to get in the game or agree to a resolution. On the principal's side, the initial selection of the dispute-resolving agent is a key instrument in the principal's struggle to maintain control. Once appointed, substantial discretion is a necessary feature of the relationship for this type of agent to perform a this task. The principal uses fair means—and sometimes foul—to influence that discretion.

1

John Milton's much younger wife Mary Powell quickly tired of him and returned to her family in 1642. He was, or he became, an early advocate of divorce. In 1643, in *The Doctrine and Discipline of Divorce*, he argued that a magistrate ought to consider not just adultery as grounds for divorce. The magistrate should consider the wider benefits of "conjugal society," and whether the parties at least could find solace and peace together. A magistrate is necessary, he argued in *The Tenure of Kings and Magistrates*, "lest each man should be his own partial Judge."[2] A man ahead of his time with his social contract theory and his views on marriage and divorce, Milton failed to resolve his personal situation with resort to an impartial magistrate. After five years, his wife returned to him. Biographers do not suggest that they found peace and solace together.[3]

---

[1] David Lake and Matthew McCubbins, "The Logic of Delegation to International Organizations," in Hawkins et al. (2006), pp. 343–344; On the trustee role, see Karen Alter, "Delegation to International Courts and the Limits of Re-contracting Political Power," in Hawkins et al. (2006), p. 334. For a nuanced defense of a principal-agent approach, see also Manfred Elsig and Mark Pollack, "Agents, Trustees and International Courts: The Politics of Judicial Appointments at the World Trade Organization," *European Journal of International Relations* 20, no. 2 (2014): 391–495.

[2] Milton ([1650] 2013), 250.

[3] Christopher Hill, *Milton and the English Revolution* (London: Faber and Faber 1977), p. 134.

To prevent a breakdown in relationships, or to set aside relationships that have broken down, we turn to agents. We authorize them to try to get us back together, or to sort out how we part. If love does not reignite under the guidance of the relationship counselor, then a court settles custody and property disputes. To cut costs, the couple may not appear before a judge in the end, but they find a way out only in the shadow of this agent.

2

Financially, the NFL does very well under the management of the commissioner, Roger Goodell. At the same time, the League's reputation takes a battering. Goodell's tasks extend beyond television deals. He decides disciplinary cases and settles disputes among the team owners. Fans, players, and even individual owners level harsh criticism at how he performs this task, and yet the owners renew his contract. A theoretically interesting feature of the commissioner's role as agent of the collective principal of team owners is his multitasking. Multitasking complicates the evaluation of an agent. Performance may vary across tasks. And tasks may be of unequal importance. For the principal, some variability in the agent's performance across tasks may still amount to successful delegation, perhaps indicated by contract renewal. With Goodell, the television deals make up for the irritation he causes the owners in arbitrating disputes and arbitrarily punishing individual players.

Thanks to his office and the constitution of the NFL, Goodell is a powerful man. He doles out unequal punishments to players in a savage game, and profits greatly (to mangle Tennyson's "Ulysses"). He can expect $200 million from his five-year contract with the team owners, who are referred to as "the Membership." He punishes them too: "Goodell serves at the Membership's pleasure and carries out their wishes, except when he is fining them, taking their draft picks away and damaging their reputations."[4] Behaving in this way, his survival surely becomes an issue? Even if, as we saw in the earlier chapter, he "manages up" and cultivates a subset of the collective principal, at some point he alienates sufficient numbers to jeopardize his contract. Yet a winning coalition of the aggrieved is yet to emerge. He carries on.

The qualifications and terms of office for the commissioner are in the NFL constitution. The owners "shall select and employ a person of unquestioned integrity to serve as Commissioner of the League."[5] There are those who question Goodell's integrity. In 2014, the National Organization for Women (NOW) called for his resignation, protesting his rulings on domestic violence by NFL players. He appeared to adjust his punishments to the size of the public outcry rather than to the gravity of the offense.

Drawing NOW's ire was Goodell's fumbling of Ray Rice's punishment. Baltimore Ravens' running back Rice and his fiancée spent Valentine's Day of 2014 in a hotel in Atlantic City. They argued in the hotel elevator. Rice knocked his fiancée unconscious with a blow to her head. He was arrested. He avoided a trial by agreeing to an "intervention program." In June 2014, the NFL commissioner met with Rice and his now wife about the assault. Reminding Rice that the NFL valued integrity and sought to maintain public confidence, he suspended Rice for two games. The punishment did not fit the violence of the crime. A teammate received a much longer suspension for smoking marijuana.[6] The Rice affair resurfaced in September 2014 with the posting of a video of the violence in the elevator. Responding to renewed outrage, the commissioner said the video was new information to him. He increased the punishment from a two-game suspension to an indefinite suspension. Goodell said Rice

---

[4] Mark Leibovich, "Roger Goodell's Unstoppable Football Machine," *New York Times*, February 3, 2016. https://www.nytimes.com/2016/02/07/magazine/roger-goodells-unstoppable-football-machine.html.

[5] Constitution and Bylaws of the National Football League ([1970] 2006), p. 28. https://www.onlabor.org/wp-content/uploads/2017/04/co_pdf.

[6] "Ray Rice's New Ravens Teammate Has Six-Game Suspension for Smoking Pot," *Los Angeles Times*, July 25, 2014. https://www.latimes.com/sports/sportsnow/la-sp-sn-ravens-will-hill-ray-rice-20140725-story.html.

misled him during the June meeting. Rice appealed. The finding was that Rice, not the commissioner, had told the truth. Not disputing the commissioner's discretion to impose punishment, as Rice had not lied to the commissioner, the indefinite suspension was deemed arbitrary.[7] In addition to his rulings on domestic violence, the commissioner attracted unwelcome attention and controversy with his suspension of a quarterback for allegedly throwing an underinflated football, which blew up in "Deflategate," and with his insouciance to the health risks of those who play the game.

Blows to their own heads inflict lasting damage on American football players. There is a link to chronic traumatic encephalopathy (CTE), a disease boxers get. A sample of brains of former players revealed that most had had the disease.[8] Goodell discussed CTE in his annual state of the game speech. *Washington Post* columnist Sally Jenkins described the speech as "defending the indefensible." Goodell suggested that even couch potatoes run health risks and said he would like his son to play the game. "If Goodell were a good, strong Commissioner," Jenkins wrote, "instead of posing as a Roman senator, he would lobby the owners to get out ahead of the health issue once and for all by leveling with players and the audience."[9] But the owners agreed with the commissioner. The Cowboys' Jerry Jones had previously dismissed the link between the disease and the game as "absurd."

Despite his inconsistency in punishing domestic violence, his questionable grasp of medical science and other issues, Goodell survives and prospers. Fans may be difficult to please. When he went to a game, New England Patriot fans took the trouble to wear T-shirts with a clown nose on the commissioner's face. All the same, Goodell receives huge financial bonuses from the Membership. The

[7] Appeal *In the Matter of Ray Rice* (November 28, 2014). https://s3.amazonaws.com/s3.documentcloud.org/documents/1372767/judge-ruling-ray-rice-decision.pdf   (accessed September 7, 2017).

[8] Anna C. McKee et al., "Clinicopathological Evaluation of Chronic Traumatic Encephalopathy in Players of American Football," *Journal of the American Medical Association* 318, no. 4 (2017): 360–370.

[9] "Roger Goodell Defends the Indefensible, Spinning Nonsense," *Washington Post*, February 5, 2016. https://www.washingtonpost.com/sports/redskins/roger-goodell-defends-the-indefensible-spinning-nonsense/2016/02/05/5d22deac-cc50-11e5-88ff-e2d1b4289c2f_story.html.

nature of the task, the incentives at work, and the characteristics of the principal help explain Goodell's survival.

3

The NFL constitution gives the commissioner enormous discretion. Beyond his authority to approve all television and broadcast contracts and handle collective bargaining agreements with the players, under the heading "Jurisdiction to Resolve Disputes" the commissioner has "full, complete, and final jurisdiction and authority to arbitrate . . . any dispute involving a member or members in the League or any players or employees of the members of the League . . . that in the opinion of the Commissioner constitutes conduct detrimental to the best interests of the League."[10] Without this delegation of authority to resolve disputes, the owners would be "partial judges" and absorbed with their individual gains and losses. Under paragraph 8.3 of the NFL Constitution, the Commissioner has authority to arbitrate disputes among owners, and under paragraph 3.11 the owners are "bound" to comply with the Commissioner's decisions. His powers to arbitrate and punish stipulate that he possesses "complete authority" to suspend or fine individuals. Given that once he is in place, a commissioner's authority may influence the fortunes of owners and the careers of their players, selection is a key control mechanism for the principal. Not knowing the character and motivations of the agent could be very costly to the principal.

With Roger Goodell, the Membership appointed a man they knew well. Goodell reportedly loves the game, played in high school, and had a prolonged try-out in lesser roles. He set his sights on being the commissioner of the NFL from an early age. He got his break in the organization as a twenty-two-year-old intern.[11] He worked his way up.

---

[10] Constitution and Bylaws of the National Football League ([1970] 2006), p. 28.

[11] "How Roger Goodell Became the Most Powerful Man in American Sports," *Washington Post*, September 3, 2015. https://www.washingtonpost.com/sports/redskins/how-roger-goodell-became-the-most-powerful-man-in-american-sports/2015/09/02/3eb69baa-50d8-11e5-9812-92d5948a40f8_story.html.

On the job, internal monitoring of the NFL commissioner is limited. It takes the form of a report submitted by the commissioner at the annual meeting of the League members. Outside the institution, on the other hand, there is great public appetite for news of the game. The media's coverage of the NFL provides a stream of more or less welcome information about the commissioner's performance. The implications for the commissioner are not straightforward. Members of the collective principal must agree on how to evaluate his performance across the different tasks he performs, and, for example, on the weight to give revenue generation or NOW's criticism of the handling of domestic violence and the reputational costs. Then the members have to coordinate their action. Despite damaging headlines, the years in office, and the sanctions he imposes on individual owners, the Membership has not acted to punish the agent. He is doing something right.

4

While there are areas of the commissioner's performance that are deeply controversial, during his tenure the financial performance of the NFL has exceeded expectations. Revenues increased dramatically coincident with Goodell becoming commissioner in 2006. The owners know the financial outcome for the NFL, although not precisely what mix of skill, diligence, and luck produced this result. Not being able to isolate an agent's contribution complicates evaluation and incentives. But if the "bottom line" is the indicator of this agent's performance, then despite the headlines, it is not so surprising that the owners extend Goodell's contract.

His task to arbitrate disputes with players and owners and so protect the reputation of the League is one that is more difficult to measure and therefore more difficult for the collective principal to agree upon a course of action. The economist Bengt Holmström describes an agent with two tasks: "One task can be perfectly measured—think about quantity sold. The other task is very hard to measure—think about the reputation of the firm. There may be some measures available for the latter, for instance consumer feedback. But such information is selective and often biased."[12] More measurable tasks, easily linked to bonuses, are likely to get the attention of the agent and the principal. Holmström picks the example of the BP Deepwater Horizon oil spill in the Gulf of Mexico. BP prioritized easy-to-measure successful exploration at the expense of hard-to-measure safety provisions for uncertain risks: "measurable results were pushed hard."[13] With a collective principal, the bias toward tasks that can be more readily and accurately measured is likely to increase. Better measurement means less internal disagreement among members over the performance of the agent. With NFL owners, the returns from sponsorships and broadcast deals are likely to be the least uncertain and least contested performance measure.

Goodell's effort is directed toward increasing these returns by lucrative bonuses that far outweigh his annual salary. As the *New York Times* pointed out, despite the highly visible domestic violence rulings, in 2014 Goodell had done well with broadcast deals and received a salary of about $4 million and over $30 million in bonuses and benefits.[14] Goodell may attract criticism in the disputes he decides on, the punishments he hands out, and the rationales he comes up with. These outcomes are tolerated. If the owners wanted it otherwise, then Goodell's incentives would be rebalanced. The incentives offered the commissioner reveal the Membership's priorities. If the performance of the arbitration task was more concerning, then theory suggests that at the risk of lowering the agent's overall effort, bonuses would be scrapped and a flat salary would encourage him to distribute his efforts more evenly among tasks. If all else fails, then they do not renew the contract. The owners do neither of these things.

His latest renewal did nonetheless expose cracks in the collective principal. The Dallas Cowboys' owner, Jerry Jones, was threatening

[12] Bengt Holmström, "Pay for Performance and Beyond," *American Economic Review* 107, no. 7 (2017): 1766.
[13] Holmström (July 2017), 1768.
[14] "Roger Goodell Said to Be in Line for New Five-Year N.F.L.Contract," *New York Times*, August 21, 2017. https://www.nytimes.com/2017/08/21/sports/football/roger-goodell-nfl-contract.html.

to block the renewal just a year after he had given a warm tribute to "classy" Roger Goodell. Jones and President Trump disagreed with Goodell's handling of national anthem demonstrations by players protesting police brutality and racial injustice. But what incensed the owner was Goodell's meting out a six-game suspension for the behavior of the Cowboys' running back Ezekiel Elliott; he was another player accused of domestic violence. The Cowboys' owner lawyered-up and blazed away. He told the commissioner, "I'm gonna come after you with everything I have," and if Goodell thought that the owner of the Patriots, Bob Kraft (who fell out with Goodell over inflated footballs), "came after you hard, Bob Kraft is a [expletive] compared to what I'm going to do."[15] A collective principal may commit to impartial judges, then once play is underway they do what they can to influence whoever is in place. The necessary discretion the agent enjoys for this task means the principal's responses are limited. Between renewal decisions, threats and smears maybe all that is available, which is why we sometimes see judges receive similar treatment. Understandably, Jerry Jones wanted to terminate the agent. But loss was concentrated, not broadly distributed across the Membership. Fellow owners did not feel his pain. They weighed the agent's performance differently, and while the Cowboys' owner managed to delay the negotiation of Goodell's new contract, he could not prevent it. It is at the pleasure of the Membership, not just as a result of his paranoia, that Goodell survives; Jerry Jones, the alienated members of the sporting public, NOW, and various media commentators may impugn but must endure, until at least 2024.

5

Day to day, Roger Goodell may be the most powerful man in American football, but he is so with the approval of the principal.

---

[15] "NFL Owners Send Jerry Jones a Message with Roger Goodell's Contract Extension," *Washington Post*, December 7, 2017. https://www.washingtonpost.com/news/early-lead/wp/2017/12/07/nfl-owners-send-jerry-jones-a-message-with-roger-goodells-contract-extension/.

In the football played by the rest of the world, Sepp Blatter won five consecutive terms as president of FIFA. He once described himself as president of everything.[16] Blatter and his predecessor, Jorge Havelange, saw FIFA become an international organization rolling in sponsorship and broadcasting money and, in contrast to the NFL, rotten with corruption. FIFA officials enriched themselves at the expense of the reputation of the game. Blatter and other officials are gone; it is unclear whether the organization has been reformed. FIFA is a story of seemingly all-powerful, multitasking agents who decide who hosts the World Cup, who create public outrage in the process, but who also serve at the pleasure of a collective principal.

Members of FIFA are football associations, one for each country. These associations form confederations, which run continent-wide competitions. FIFA's "supreme and legislative body" is the yearly Congress. The associations vote for the president by secret ballot for a four-year term. In 2010, a twenty-four-person Executive Committee, made up of the president, eight vice presidents, and fifteen members appointed by the member associations and confederations, chose Qatar as the 2022 host country of the World Cup. It was an improbable decision that engulfed that state and the organization in scandal.

Qatar is a country of two million people, without a large football fan base, and with a climate that is too hot for a summer tournament. A winter World Cup conflicts with the players' professional club schedules. Fans will sit in a stadium built by exploited migrants, according to Amnesty International's report on Qatar's "World Cup of Shame." If their team disappoints, they will be unable to drown their sorrows. Alcohol is hard to find. Sober thoughts may turn to the corruption that brought them and the Cup to Doha.

The storm gathered in 2015. Blatter, in his 2015 presidential acceptance speech, described FIFA as a boat returning to shore. He was

---

[16] For excellent recent accounts of FIFA, see David Conn, *The Fall of the House of FIFA* (London: Yellow Jersey Press, 2017); and Heidi Blake and Jonathan Calvert, *The Ugly Game: The Qatari Plot to Buy the World Cup* (London: Simon & Schuster, 2015). For an alternative approach to systemic corruption, see Anna Persson, Bo Rothstein, and Jan Teorell, "Why Anticorruption Reforms Fail: Systemic Corruption as a Collective Action Problem," *Governance: An International Journal of Policy, Administration, and Institutions* 26, no. 3 (2013): 449–471.

at the helm. It was a strange, desperate address feeding into journalistic accounts of an out-of-control, even out-of-touch-agent. Just launched on another four-year term, days later he went overboard in the wake of the arrest of members of FIFA's executive committee at a Zurich hotel. He seemed to have foreseen the end as early as December 2010; yet he was unprepared. Looking back and dropping his nautical metaphor, he said: "I felt like a boxer who was just going into round 12 and said I'm going to win. But then: BONG!"[17] Bonged and banned from football, Blatter escaped arrest.

Qatar was the knockout blow. He and over half of the FIFA Executive Committee, the body that decided on the World Cup of shame, were in trouble. They were banned, found guilty of racketeering, indicted, or under investigation for corruption. The onset of rot at FIFA is traced to a German businessman, Horst Dassler of Adidas, whom Blatter worked for before joining FIFA in 1975, and whose sports marketing company's bankruptcy in 2001 revealed the bribes paid to FIFA officials.[18] Selecting an insider like Blatter as president suggested that those in charge were uninterested in reform.

FIFA's most visible function is to decide among bids to hold the World Cup. FIFA officials took bribes from the bidders. The US Federal Bureau of Investigation (FBI) caught up with New Yorker Charles Blazer, a member of FIFA's Executive Committee. He pleaded guilty to racketeering conspiracy, income tax evasion, and other charges in 2013 and informed on his FIFA colleagues.

Bribes did not always work, nor were they the only private benefit sought by officials. Morocco reportedly distributed bribes to influence the 1998 and 2010 tournaments. Those tournaments went to France and South Africa. As for the mechanics of the bribes, a delegate from the Ivory Coast said that Qatar had offered members $1 million plus for "projects" in return for votes on the 2022 decision,

---

[17] "Lunch with the FT: Sepp Blatter," *Financial Times*, October 30, 2015. https://www.ft.com/content/5457de04-7e48-11e5-a1fe-567b37f80b64.

[18] "The £66m 'Bribe' Shadow Hanging over FIFA," *The Telegraph*, March 13, 2008. https://www.telegraph.co.uk/sport/columnists/davidbond/2294323/The-66m-bribe-shadow-hanging-over-Fifa.html.

with a third down ahead of the vote and the rest on a successful out-come.[19] But it was not money alone motivating the agents. As we know, agents' motives can be more obscure. Social cachet as well as cash guided FIFA decisions. In the run-up to the South Africa de-cision, FIFA official Jack Warner held out for a personal visit from Nelson Mandela and Desmond Tutu.[20] While Blatter had been sym-pathetic at one stage, he was unhappy with Qatar. He supported the US bid. Blatter told *Financial Times* journalist Malcolm Moore of an agreement among FIFA "leaders" that the 2018 and 2022 World Cup competitions would go to the two superpowers: "it was behind the scenes. It was diplomatically arranged to go there."[21] Blatter's eyes were on the Nobel Peace Prize. He received encouragement for "par-ticular recognition" from the 2018 host country president, Vladimir Putin.[22]

The World Cup generates huge revenues. FIFA distributes the proceeds among member associations. For many associations, these distributions pay their officials and build their facilities. Journalists Heidi Blake and Jonathan Calvert describe Blatter's financial schemes to "reward supporters," the lavish treatment of members of the Executive Committee, and estimate that some 75 percent of the associations relied on huge dispensations from FIFA.[23] If 75 percent of the associations benefited, then they had a powerful incentive to put up with Blatter and his colorful crew.

If not dependent on FIFA disbursements and seeking finan-cial gain, fear of retribution kept a minority of national football associations in line. Not wishing to jeopardize their dreams of hosting a World Cup, the English Football Association looked the other way. In 2010, the Association called a BBC program that

---

[19] House of Commons, "Written Evidence Submitted by the *Sunday Times*," *Culture, Media and Sport Committee*, May 9, 2011. https://publications.parliament.uk/pa/cm201012/cmselect/cmcumeds/1031/1031we02.htm.

[20] "Morocco Threat Sends Mandela into Action," *The Telegraph*, May 6, 2004. https://www.telegraph.co.uk/sport/2378290/Morocco-threat-sends-Mandela-into-action.html.

[21] "Lunch with the FT: Sepp Blatter" (2015). https://www.ft.com/content/5457de04-7e48-11e5-a1fe-567b37f80b64.

[22] "Vladimir Putin Thinks FIFA's Blatter Deserves a Nobel Prize," *Fortune*, July 28, 2015. https://fortune.com/2015/07/28/vladimir-putin-thinks-fifas-blatter-deserves-a-nobel-prize/.

[23] Blake and Calvert (2015).

exposed FIFA officials' corruption "an embarrassment."[24] Yet they knew the BBC account was accurate. It was consistent with their interactions with the FIFA Executive Committee. All the same, the English Association condemned the media, not the corruption. Like the Qataris, and if on the cheap, they agreed to improper requests. In comparison to what was on offer from Qatar, or what had been paid by South Africa to host the 2010 World Cup, the English inducements of dinners and jobs for FIFA officials' relatives were trivial, but they were a barometer of the pressure exerted by agents with the authority to decide among the bidders.[25] Unsuccessful if not unsullied, the English hid knowledge of the corruption, until they lost. They did not blow the whistle and they denigrated those that did.

6

In trying to understand what went wrong at FIFA, attention was on Blatter and his peculiarities: "On the one hand he has a complex of inferiority, related probably to his body size. He's a small fellow. He needs to establish himself and prove himself. And on the other hand he's very much someone who likes to stand in the centre of attention—so he looks for the platform. And he's extremely hungry for power."[26] Yet FIFA's problem is not the rogue behavior of this individual.

Counterfactually, principal-agent theory helps us think about what did not happen, as well what did happen, if the collective

---

[24] "World Cup 2018: Panorama 'Embarrassment to BBC," *The Telegraph*, November 30, 2010. https://www.telegraph.co.uk/sport/football/teams/england/8169685/World-Cup-2010-Uefa-president-Michel-Platini-suggests-BBCs-Panorama-program-should-not-harm-Englands-bid.html.

[25] SeeMichael Garcia, "Report on the Inquiry into the 2018/2022 FIFA World Cup Bidding Process" (2014). http://www.fifa.com/governance/news/y=2017/m=6/news=fifa-statement-on-recent-media-coverage-regarding-the-garcia-report-2898791.html (accessed November 24, 2017); James Dingemans, "Review of the Allegations of Misconduct in Relation to the FA's 2018 World Cup Bid" (2011). http://www.FIFA.com/mm/document/affederation/adminis-tration/01/44/40/85/jdqcreview-summary.pdf (accessed November 7, 2017).

[26] "FIFA Corruption Crisis: Who Does Sepp Blatter Think He Is?," BBC, May 28, 2015. http://www.bbc.co.uk/sport/football/32925186 (accessed November 7, 2017).

principal wanted to assert control over its agent. FIFA's Executive Committee attracted individuals seeking assorted private gains. But the organization made no attempt to reveal these character attributes and to screen for fit and proper agents. While the FIFA Congress could challenge an appointment, it did not exercise this power.[27] Congress repeatedly re-contracted Blatter. The national associations did not use the mechanisms available to control their president and other agents on the Executive Committee. On the contrary, they repeatedly endorsed their actions, even after the FBI's intervention. There was no information asymmetry about the corruption of the officials, and there were mechanisms in place to hold officials accountable. The fact is the associations did not engage these mechanisms.

With the collective principal composed of national associations, two factors, loss and gain, are at work. First, for some members of the collective principal, the perceived cost of taking control may have been too high and the probability of success too remote. Some, like the English Football Association in 2010, pretended not to know about corruption. The high stakes encouraged member associations with bids or prospective bids to go along and not sound the alarm or silence the alarm when it did sound. Second, the majority of members of the collective principal, without ambition to host the next World Cup, benefited from the efforts of Blatter and others in the form of revenue flows. For them, there was not a principal-agent problem (that an agent is acting immorally or illegally does not mean he is out of control). They kept re-contracting him. Performing on this easy-to-measure task, Blatter and his FIFA officials carried on. These gains and fear of losses kept the associations on board and Blatter afloat.

While the media may point to the rottenness at the top of FIFA, and while the personalities involved may encourage this interpretation of events, it is a mistake to take these accounts at face value. Blatter only seemed to have grown, Frankenstein-like, beyond the

---

[27] See Garcia, "Report on the Inquiry into the 2018/2022 FIFA World Cup Bidding Process" (2014).

control of the organization that gave birth to his very public life. But Blatter served at the pleasure of the collective principal. He emerged from deep inside the organization to be appointed to the top position. The sports-loving public may view him with horror. But from the collective principal's perspective, it is successful delegation. It may not work for most of the rest of us, but it worked for the national associations and it worked for Blatter and the Executive Committee. They served repeated terms.

Given this structure and these incentives, it is not surprising that FIFA did not fix itself. Only a shocking intervention by a superior external authority offered a way out. Ironically, and necessarily, it came from a country that cared less about the game. It was not Switzerland, where FIFA is headquartered, that tried to put things right. As Christopher Bourdreaux, Gokhan Karahan, and R. Morris Coats point out, Switzerland "has more to lose than it does to gain if it actually supervises FIFA. For instance, if Switzerland attempts to monitor FIFA, its soccer team(s) may possibly be penalized in the future by FIFA."[28] It was the United States that took the lead in holding the FIFA officials accountable. On May 27, 2015, Attorney General Loretta Lynch, FBI Director James Comey, and other officials announced the indictment on racketeering conspiracy and corruption charges of nine top FIFA officials and five sports marketing executives. That May morning, Swiss authorities arrested seven of the defendants at a Zurich hotel. Guilty pleas had already been obtained from other FIFA officials.

FIFA reforms in 2016 transferred the decision on the hosting of the World Cup to the Congress as a whole. There is now a "Review Committee" with independent members to carry out "eligibility checks" on FIFA officials. Despite these changes, the chain of delegation stretches through continental confederations, which retain control of the seats on the Council, and then to the national member associations. The delegates who constitute the Congress are not screened, and, according to Miguel Maduro, who was briefly the

---

[28] Christopher J. Boudreaux, Gokhan Karahan, and R. Morris Coats, "Bend It like FIFA: Corruption on and off the Pitch," *Managerial Finance* 42, no. 9 (2016): 868.

chair of the FIFA Governance Committee, there is little improvement in the way confederations are run and the way the confederations allocate their seats on the Council.[29] In office for just ten months, in May 2017, Maduro was removed by Congress on the recommendation of President Gianni Infantino. Maduro had attempted to screen some FIFA officials. The chairs of the Ethics and Adjudicatory Committees were also dismissed by Congress. Other independent members of the Governance Committee resigned in protest, including former UN High Commissioner of Human Rights, Navi Pillay. According to Maduro, Blatter's successor valued his political survival as president over reform. While not using these terms, Maduro traced the problem back to the collective principal: "there is a culture in the institution that starts at the level of the football associations and the confederations. . . . That culture is extremely resistant to accountability, independent scrutiny, transparency and the prevention of conflicts of interest."[30] The decision to remove Maduro and the others passed with *98 percent* of the vote in Congress.

We cannot expect change coming from within the delegation relationship. In line with this analysis, Professor Maduro stated to the House of Commons that reform of FIFA will only come about from the outside. In terms of outside actors—indicating the scale of the challenge with an international organization dependent on the over 200 largely ungoverned national associations—he thought only the United States or the European Union large enough to exercise the necessary pressure. If, for example, Professor Maduro's Portugal alone decided to do something, it would be punished by FIFA, he intimated.

7

The authority granted agents in this type of delegation relationship provokes doubt about the relevance of principal-agent theory, although

---

[29] House of Commons, "Professor Miguel Maduro Oral Evidence: Sports Governance," *Digital, Culture, Media and Sport Committee*, HC 320, September 13, 2017.
[30] House of Commons (2017), 3.

rather than the sporting life, the empirical focus is judges sitting on international courts. It is true that the delegation relationship to resolve disputes reduces the repertoire of control mechanisms readily available to the principal and the timeliness with which they can be applied. An option, between selection and reselection of this agent, is to resort to invective, which was the Cowboys' approach to Goodell when he ruled on the domestic abuse case. Generally, the principal is not able to manage this agent from dispute to dispute with bonuses and sackings. It would seem improper if she did. Indeed, this effort to bias specific decisions, usually with some money down and then more when the outcome was known, was the FIFA approach. With this task, the principal has to look for agents with similar preferences and hope for the best.

As Jerry Jones delayed Goodell's contract renewal negotiations, the United States is using the appointment process in the struggle to influence the Appellate Body of the World Trade Organization (WTO). The Appellate Body of the WTO is appointed by the member states. It is where the United States makes the case against Mexican tuna, New Zealand lamb, or wheat gluten from the European Union. Its judges, or the commissioner of the NFL for that matter, at times disappoint members of their respective collective principals, whether the United States or the owner of the Dallas Cowboys. The discretion of this agent is part of the game-initiating bargain which induces the parties to get involved. There would be little reason for Mexico to join the WTO in the first place if they knew their tuna was a loser.

If an Appellate Body judge does not perform to the liking of the principal, then they may not get re-nominated. With the WTO about to investigate US tariffs on Chinese exports, the Trump administration claimed that the Appellate Body had gone rogue, and began blocking the appointment of judges to this body. Other members of the collective principal—sixty-seven member states— have petitioned the United States to stop vetoing the process.[31] It may be that the WTO needs reform, but in blocking the delegation

[31] "U.S. Blocks WTO Judge Reappointment as Dispute Settlement Crisis Looms," *Reuters*, August 27, 2018. https://uk.reuters.com/article/uk-usa-trade-wto/u-s-blocks-wto-judge-reappointment-as-dispute-settlement-crisis-looms-idUKKCN1LC19G.

route, the United States is opting for disagreement and trade war and presumably is willing to risk other countries using unfair trade practices against US exporters, rather than peace and intermittent solace from dispute resolution.

The high stakes involved in resolving some disputes may raise the issue of whether deciding to not delegate is a serious option. It might be a bluff with the WTO, but with FIFA and its task of deciding on World Cup bids, there are alternatives to delegation. For example, a lottery among countries that meet some stadium and infrastructure threshold has been suggested.[32] For the NFL, as the principal-agent literature suggests, it is worth itemizing the tasks and considering what to assign to agents. Here, more delegation in the form of different agents for the commissioner's different tasks—separating dispute resolution from revenue generation—might be an alternative.

Finally, the salience of the appointment process as a mechanism of control for the dispute-resolving agent does not make for a special agent, operating beyond the theory. A general theme, as we saw in the previous chapter with the church and the army, is the potency of selection and knowing the preferences of the agent. Although these agents may appear to possess "imperious" authority, it is worth attending to the range of tasks they perform and the behavior of the principal. The agent may appear very grand. The decisions of the agent may be controversial. They may be corrupt. Yet if we attend to the logic of delegation, we may discover that the agent is not out of control.

---

[32] "A Radical Idea: Hold an Auction to Decide the World Cup Hosts to Stop Corruption," *The Guardian*, April 30, 2018. https://www.theguardian.com/football/2018/apr/30/world-cup-highest-bidder.

5
Commitment

We tie our hands, or ourselves to a mast like Ulysses, to resist passing fancies. Sometimes we need saving from ourselves, lacking self-control. The examples are familiar. We give someone else the keys to the drink cabinet, affirming a New Year's resolution. We rely on the agent, deaf to entreaties, to keep us on the road to health and happiness. At other times, we are perfectly able to control ourselves. The problem is that others are skeptical. Has he really given up the bottle? We delegate in order to affirm our commitment to a partner, wife, or some other valued audience. Also worth a thought is the insincere principal, lacking real resolve. He delegates his commitment to a weak agent in order to dupe the valued audience.

Decision-makers wrestle with inconsistent preferences in personal and public life. Economists Richard Thaler and H. M. Shefrin develop a principal-agent model of a "two-self economic man," with a personality split between a consumer and a saver. Young, wealthy pro-athletes provide an extreme example of this disorder. Looking for a way out, "some athletes hire agents to invest their incomes and limit their current spending."[1] Scaling up from Thaler and Shefrin's "economic theory of self-control" to the national level, political leaders may be torn between power and principle. A president may have commitments to price stability, to human rights, and to protecting the environment, which are all highly worthy goals for the long term. The difficulty is she also wants an uptick in the economy, improved public support, and to win an election. To preserve the integrity of agreed-upon economic or other goals and to put limits on

---

[1] Richard H. Thaler and H. M. Shefrin, "An Economic Theory of Self-Control," *Journal of Political Economy* 89, no. 2 (1981): 392–406; see also Jon Elster, *Ulysses and the Sirens* (Cambridge: Cambridge University Press, 1984).

Why Delegate?. Neil J. Mitchell, Oxford University Press (2021). © Oxford University Press.
DOI: 10.1093/oso/9780190904197.003.0005

current spending, politicians hand over the policy keys to those who are beyond temptation. They delegate to central banks and domestic and international agencies. A two-self economic person struggles with spending today or saving for an easy retirement. A "two-goal political leader" struggles with a boost to the economy today or long-term policy commitments and an easy national conscience.

In 2018, the United Kingdom agreed to sell forty-eight war planes to Saudi Arabia. Recall that Saudi Arabia had attracted widespread criticism for the murder of Jamal Khashoggi as well as for bombing Yemen. In contrast to the United Kingdom, Germany, which makes components for the war planes, denied arms export licenses to Saudi Arabia in response to the Khashoggi killing, leading to a dispute with the British government. The British government chose economic performance, framed in the principled terms of a NATO commitment, over human rights commitments. British foreign minister Jeremy Hunt wrote to Germany's foreign minister: "I am very concerned about the impact of the German government's decision on the British and European defence industry and the consequences for Europe's ability to fulfil its NATO commitments."[2] Perhaps Angela Merkel's government aside, leaders have difficulty, on their own, controlling their short-term self-interest and making heroic choices that risk their public support. To affirm a policy commitment, they can shift responsibility for, say, the management of monetary policy, or the monitoring and enforcement of human rights protections (but not arms export licenses) to domestic or international agencies.

As a commitment device, delegation allows the agent discretion in order to keep a principal to her commitment. As with the agent who resolves disputes, the agent who looks after our commitments may have substantial independent authority. The intent behind this authority is not to act at the expense of the principal, or at least of the principal's "better self." The premise for this delegation is the split preferences of the principal. The agent represents one of these

---

[2] "German Halt in Saudi Arms Sales Hurting UK Industry—Hunt," *Reuters*, February 19, 2019. https://uk.reuters.com/article/uk-germany-saudi/hunt-german-halt-in-saudi-arms-sales-to-hit-british-defence-industry-report-idUKKCN1Q81SF.

preferences; he is an ally of her "long-term" self, if you like.[3] Tension builds in this delegation relationship as the agent delivers on the commitment, particularly where the principal was naïve about the challenge posed by the commitment, as sometimes happens with New Year's Resolutions. Or tension builds in the relationship if the agent tries to deliver and the "two-faced" principal, who used delegsation insincerely to affirm to others a commitment she does not genuinely hold, regrets the arrangement when the commitment bites. Not all commitments are sincerely given. Handing over the keys to the drinks cabinet or the economy or for that matter the tools of repression may turn out to be a weak commitment device, designed to reassure others, but of symbolic rather than practical effect.

1

Almost 80 percent of NFL players are broke five years after retiring, so *Sports Illustrated* sensationally claimed in 2009. A more systematic and more conservative analysis found that bankruptcy filings among NFL players begin soon after retirement and rise to one in six within twelve years, which is still a bankruptcy rate much higher than comparison groups in the general population on lower incomes.[4] A sybaritic lifestyle, perhaps just reward for the savage game, is accessorized with an entourage of long-lost friends and untrustworthy advisers, often family members. A high divorce rate compounds the emotional and financial hazards for ex-players.

An alternative to personal boom and bust is to find someone to smooth your consumption. David Heide of Heide Wealth Management helps pro-athletes watch their spending: "I have

---

[3] For a somewhat different view, see Miller and Whitford, *Above Politics* (2015); Bendor et al. (2001); Fabrizio Gilardi, *Delegation in the Regulatory State: Independent Regulatory Agencies in Western Europe* (Cheltenham, UK: Edward Elgar, 2008).

[4] Kyle Carlson, Joshua Kim, Annamaria Lusard, and Colin F. Camerer, "Bankruptcy Rates among NFL Players with Short-Lived Income Spikes," *American Economic Review* 105, no. 5 (2015): 381–384.

clients that need $500 a month from me. . . . If you're getting $20,000 a month from me, you have to have a portfolio of $6 million. . . . I gotta sleep at night too and know that my recommendations for the long term are going to work."[5] According to Heide, an important part of his task is helping players resist strange requests to invest in restaurants. The NFL Players Association offers financial education and a list of trusted financial advisors to help overcome the selection problem players face in finding an agent and in order to impose some control over their "spending self."

2

Moving up from managing personal finances to the nation's finances and to affirm that the economy is in good hands to skeptical investors, borrowers, and voters, politicians delegate to those insulated from election pressures. Independent central bankers have wax in their ears when the politicians who appointed them call for an election fillip.

The United States Federal Reserve implements monetary policy. Its objectives are a sound economy, strong employment, and financial stability. Its key officials, the Board of Governors, are nominated by the president and confirmed by the Senate. The chair and vice chair have four-year renewable terms. The Federal Reserve's decisions on interest rates affect spending, investment, exchange rates, stock prices, and employment. With this influence and with the importance of the economy to voters, it is not surprising that the preferences of presidents and those on the Open Market Committee of the Federal Reserve diverge from time to time. This divergence only rarely becomes public for fear of creating alarm among investors about the independence of the bank.

Looking back, President George H. W. Bush blamed Federal Reserve Chairman Alan Greenspan for losing the 1992 election: "I

---

[5] "How to Manage Your Money like . . . a Pro Athlete?" *The Guardian*, February 2, 2014. https://www.theguardian.com/money/2014/feb/02/manage-sports-pro-athlete-investment-saving.

reappointed him, and he disappointed me."[6] President Trump appointed Federal Reserve Chairman Jerome Powell and quickly registered his disappointment with "a gentleman that likes raising interest rates in the Fed."[7] He wanted to fire him. President Trump is not alone. Other "populist" political leaders, highly dependent on public support, find difficulty keeping to commitments held by central banks. They pressure the banks, and they do so with some success. For example in 2019, Narendra Modi who "burnt his way through two central bank governors," got an interest rate cut before the election, and President Erdogan got a boost prior to municipal elections in Turkey.[8] The economist Kenneth Rogoff points to the inflationary downside of undermining a central banker's independence: "those countries that do that, including the US, will live to regret it."[9] The US Federal Reserve's multiple principal setup, with the Senate confirming the nomination, constrains a president's choices. Its longevity provides further insulation from direct political pressure. Yet the robustness of even such a venerable commitment device is shaped by the selection decisions and resilience of the actors involved.

Governments delegate not only to domestic agencies and individuals, but also to international organizations in order to affirm their commitment to good governance. We can understand the formation of international organizations such as the United Nations Human Rights Council or multilateral international aid agencies as a delegation by sovereign states to affirm their commitments. While central banks are standard fare for principal-agent theorists, human rights provide a particularly interesting illustration. It is a commitment that elicits skepticism

---

[6] "Trump Takes a Rare Presidential Swipe at the Fed," *New York Times*. July 19, 2018. https://www.nytimes.com/2018/07/19/business/trump-fed-interest-rates.html.

[7] "All the Trump Quotes on Powell," *Bloomberg*, March 4, 2019. https://www.bloomberg.com/news/articles/2019-08-22/key-trump-quotes-on-powell-as-fed-remains-in-the-firing-line.

[8] "Small Wonder Central Banks Find their Independence under Threat," *Daily Telegraph*, April 24, 2019. https://www.telegraph.co.uk/business/2019/04/24/small-wonder-central-banks-including-bank-england-find-independence/.

[9] "Trump's Attacks on the Fed Trigger Global Alarm," *Financial Times*, April 14, 2019. https://www.ft.com/content/3f756b5e-5e10-11e9-b285-3acd5d43599e.

in the light of states' often incompatible selfish, more short-term, strategic self.

3

If a government choosing to tie down the inflationary urge is remarkable, what about tying down the repressive urge? Does the lion lie down with the lamb? Jealously guarding sovereignty and with more or less pressing security priorities, why would political leaders create international institutions designed to tie the hands of their security forces? Why do states delegate authority over the treatment of their citizens to international institutions? Or, as the United Nations Special Rapporteur on Torture, Nigel Rodley, asked: "Why do states give us these whips to flagellate themselves with?"[10] Violence is the property of a state. Its legitimate exercise is what differentiates the state. So why put limits on its exercise? And what is the strength of this commitment device?

In 1998, under Prime Minister Tony Blair's Labour government, the United Kingdom became a state party to the Rome Treaty that set up the International Criminal Court (ICC). The Blair government affirmed its ethical foreign policy pledge. The ICC is empowered as the court of last resort, where British investigations of war crimes by its soldiers fall short of the legal standard. A decade or so later, Blair may have had second thoughts about a seemingly naively assumed commitment. The ICC launched a preliminary investigation of allegations of war crimes against British soldiers that Blair had sent to Iraq.

Acting on its second thoughts in 2017, Burundi, which ratified the Rome Statute in 2004, withdrew its commitment and revoked the authority it had granted the court. Responding to election violence in Burundi, the ICC prosecutor, Fatou Bensouda, previously had warned "high level" officials in that country that she was

---

[10] Quoted in Beth Simmons, *Mobilizing for Human Rights* (Cambridge, UK: Cambridge University Press, 2009), p. 57.

ready to take action against them. In delegating to international courts, agencies, and human rights treaty bodies, governments affirm more or less deeply held human rights commitments to domestic and foreign audiences by ostensibly giving up repression. But they may have difficulty reconciling this delegation with other priorities.

As David Lake and Matthew McCubbins and others point out, a key incentive for states to delegate to international organizations is to enhance the credibility of commitments.[11] The desire to affirm a human rights commitment may result from the internal convictions of the government of the day, or more instrumentally it may form with a valued audience in mind and in anticipation of reputational or material rewards. For example, states give up the death penalty and make commitments under the European Convention on Human Rights as preconditions for joining the European Union. If it is a reward that they are after, states may agree to this delegation also in the expectation that it will be a weak commitment device. Significantly, the Rome Statute that established the ICC has turned out to be a stronger commitment device than other human rights conventions and stronger than some states may have expected. Predictably, it has substantially fewer state parties than the major human rights treaties. In addition to Burundi, Russia withdrew its signature in 2016 (like the United States, it signed but never ratified the Statute) and the Philippines under President Duterte left the ICC in March 2019. Two general features of delegation at the international level influence the resolve and the resources of these agents and tend to make for weak commitment devices. States retain varying degrees of control over appointments to these agencies and so influence the enthusiasm and effort with which the agency delivers on its task. If they have the resolve, these international agencies may lack adequate resources independent of state actors to keep defaulters and backsliders in line. Even with a determined prosecutor, the ICC relies on state actors to enforce its decisions.

---

[11] David Lake and Matthew McCubbins, "The Logic of Delegation to International Organizations," in Hawkins et al. (2006).

4

Whether protecting human rights is a genuine conviction or not, the establishment of an international human rights regime reflects a transformation of values and a shift in what is perceived as acceptable behavior. Understanding where the attractiveness of this commitment came from takes us beyond delegation theory. Leaders were not always troubled, even in a token way, by the mayhem and violence of their followers. While slavery or sexual violence continue, unlike Homer, we know it is wrong. Agamemnon, quarrelling with Achilles over the possession of a slave girl, motivated his Greeks with "wives" over the walls of Troy. In contrast, by the Thirty Years' War, the Dutch legal theorist Hugo Grotius was condemning rape, albeit with limited effect. As we saw in a previous chapter, a soldier's conduct may lag behind a state's promises, but in recent decades the ratification of treaties marks the near universal acceptance of the idea of human rights.

The human rights commitment "offer" attracts a mix of states. The collective principal of member states has varied and inconsistent preferences in authorizing the international human rights regime. Along with those motivated to do the right thing, there will be those in the collective principal seeking to placate dissent or attract material benefits, and not expecting the collectively instructed agent to have the resolve and resources to keep them to their promises. Such a commitment signal is perceived as low cost and is rewarded with investment, trade, or aid. Human rights norms are now embedded in international economic arrangements and agreements. Recent evidence on foreign direct investment flows suggests that the decision to participate in the human rights regime and to ratify human rights conventions, irrespective of whether there is an actual improvement in human rights conditions, has a positive effect on these flows, notably for countries with poor human rights records.[12] On

---

[12] Ana C. Garriga, "Human Rights Regimes, Reputation, and Foreign Direct Investment," *International Studies Quarterly* 60, no. 1 (2016): 160–172, https://doi.org/10.1093/isq/sqw006. Empirical findings are mixed on the benefits of ratification. See Richard A. Nielsen and Beth A Simmons, "Rewards for Ratification: Payoffs for Participating in the International Human Rights Regime?," *International Studies Quarterly* 59, no. 2 (2015): 197–208, https://doi.org/

the other side of this economic relationship, investors are content to see a state's treaty ratification, irrespective of its human rights performance. It affirms the propriety of their investment decision.

If the ratifying state anticipates some future need for repression, it does not expect to be tripped up by its agents raising treaty commitments. Governments know that most abuses of human rights norms go unnoticed. If noticed, they go unpunished. Human rights agencies lack enforcement tools. The agencies rely on the cooperation of other members of the collective principal. Aid and trade sanctions are controlled by the member states of the collective principal. As the United Kingdom demonstrates in its relationship with Saudi Arabia, in general these states do not want to absorb the disproportionate costs of keeping other governments to the commitments they have made to their people. States are willing to punish other states for not fulfilling trade treaty obligations; that noncompliance has a direct impact on the punisher's well-being. But member states have less incentive to punish noncompliance with human rights treaties, where the beneficiaries are the vulnerable in faraway places who do not vote.

5

The Charter of the United Nations has the promotion of human rights among its goals. The UN established the Commission on Human Rights to set standards and "whip" noncompliant states into line. In delegating authority to this organization, governments have a dilemma. They delegate for credibility. The more latitude given the agent and the stronger the agent's human rights preferences, the greater the gain in credibility. But gains in human rights credibility may conflict with strategic preferences. State actors want credibility, not captivity by the better angels of our nature. They do not want a

10.1111/isqu.12142. See also Wade Cole, "Sovereignty Relinquished? Explaining Commitment to the International Human Rights Covenants, 1966–1999," *American Sociological Review* 70, no. 3 (2005): 472–495.

"runaway agent." Balancing gains in credibility against losses in sovereign control drives the design and performance of the agencies of the international human rights regime and the quality of human rights protection. The selection and staffing of the agencies poses the question of what balance to strike. How it is resolved indicates the strength of the principal's commitment.

The character of the agents selected is key to successful delegation and the credibility of the commitment. If the collective principal was committed to human dignity, equal moral worth, and wanted the better angels in control then the Commission would be composed of qualified and informed experts in human rights. If the principal's strategic self was in command and it wanted to tie the hands of its security forces less tightly, then the Commission would be made up of state representatives, valuing state sovereignty.

For those wanting protection for human dignity and the inalienable rights to life and liberty, it did begin well. A distinguished group made up the Commission. Former First Lady Eleanor Roosevelt, French jurist and Nobel Peace Prize winner René Cassin, and other members of the Commission drafted the Universal Declaration of Human Rights that condemned "barbarous acts that have shocked the conscience of mankind." In thirty articles, it offered individuals protection from these acts. It was a remarkable achievement in setting a common standard of human rights protection for governments around the world. It was not matched by the Commission's subsequent record in delivering human rights protection. After this brilliant launch, provisions made for the selection of the ongoing membership of the Commission signaled the trajectory it would take.

From London to Moscow, the idea of an international organization run by experts committed to human rights was seen as a threat to the sovereignty of member states.[13] Instead, the choice was for a Commission composed of fifty-three representatives of member

[13] See Paul Gordon Lauren, "To Preserve and Build on Its Achievements and to Redress Its Shortcomings: The Journey from the Commission on Human Rights to the Human Rights Council," *Human Rights Quarterly* 29, no. 2 (2007): 314.

states, elected by the UN's Economic and Social Council, serving three-year terms. Places were allocated in such a way as to ensure that this international body was geographically representative. States with poor human rights records had an incentive to get their representatives selected and so to have some more direct control of how the agency performed its task of promoting human rights.[14] Howard Tolley described regional groupings on the Commission protecting neighbors from scrutiny, whether it was African states protecting Idi Amin's Uganda, or the Soviet bloc protecting some East European violator.[15] Nevertheless, the Commission did provide some human rights benefits. States with poor human rights records had a higher probability of attracting the Commission's attention, and in the post–Cold War period of being targeted and even punished by public resolutions shaming their behavior.[16] Given the makeup of the Commission, with its moral mandate but its members situated in a political world and with their actions subject to the pressures of other goals and strategic alignments, it is perhaps surprising that there was any consistency in its shaming of repressive states.

Yet by 2005, UN Secretary General Kofi Annan had had enough. In his view, the Commission's sessions were too short to support effective monitoring of human rights performance worldwide. What time it had, the Commission devoted disproportionately to punishing Israel. Annan described the Commission as an institution used by member states to evade accountability for their own human rights violations and to criticize others. He argued that it was not up to the job. The Commission's membership included representatives from states that were notorious for human rights abuses. In 2003, Colonel Gaddafi's Libya chaired the Commission. In a moment that put the collective principal on its mettle, the United States requested a vote on Libya chairing the Commission. Of the fifty-three

---

[14] Ibid., p. 322.

[15] Howard Tolley, "The Concealed Crack in the Citadel: The United Nations Commission on Human Rights' Response to Confidential Communications," *Human Rights Quarterly* 6, no. 4 (1984): 454–455.

[16] See James H. Lebovic and Erik Voeten, "The Politics of Shame: The Condemnation of Country Human Rights Practices in the UNCHR," *International Studies Quarterly* 50, no. 4 (2006): 861–888.

members, thirty-three countries voted in favor of Libya chairing the Commission. Only two other countries voted with the United States (European countries abstained). Research suggests that member states are reluctant to punish commitment "backsliders," notably when they have strategic value.[17] Libya might be a pariah, but it had oil.

In 2005, the Commission slid too far. Robert Mugabe's Zimbabwe was re-elected to this agency. If the incentive for delegation to the Commission was advancing the credibility of human rights commitments, by 2005 it was doing the reverse. Annan was explicit about the failure of delegation: "We have reached a point at which the Commission's declining credibility has cast a shadow on the reputation of the United Nations system."[18] With his leadership, and the support of 170 member states of the United Nations, the collective principal revoked the Commission's authority. It was replaced by the Human Rights Council.

While seats continue to be allocated to the new agency on a regional basis, the Human Rights Council's forty-seven members are directly elected by the UN General Assembly for three-year terms. There was some effort to address the human rights qualifications of those chosen to serve. To screen and select the candidates for this institution, General Assembly members are instructed to seek information on the human rights credentials of the particular state. Relevant screening information includes the human rights conventions to which a state is a party, the timeliness of a state's reports to treaty bodies, and how a state approaches civil society. Once chosen, members of the Human Rights Council pledge to uphold the highest standards in protecting human rights.

Has this reform enhanced credibility? What of the human rights screening and the selection issue? Do those appointed represent

---

[17] See Inken von Borzyskowski and Felicity Vabulas "Credible Commitments? Explaining IGO Suspensions to Sanction Political Backsliding," *International Studies Quarterly* 63, no. 1 (2019): 139–152. .

[18] "Without Reform of Human Rights Body, UN Credibility at Stake, Annan Says," UN News, April 7, 2005. https://news.un.org/en/story/2005/04/134122-without-reform-human-rights-body-un-credibility-stake-annan-says.

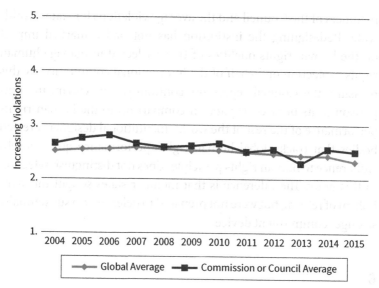

Figure 5.1. Human rights performance of the states represented on the Commission (2004–2006) and Human Rights Council (2007–2015).

states with better human rights records than those who served on the Commission?[19] For those concerned about human rights, it is difficult to detect substantial change for the better.

Figure 5.1 includes the last three years of the Commission on Human Rights and nine years of the Human Rights Council.[20] It plots average human rights violations for the fifty-three states with representatives on the Commission and for the forty-seven

[19] Mark Gibney, Linda Cornett, Reed Wood, Peter Haschke, and Daniel Arnon, *The Political Terror Scale 1976–2015* (2015). http://www.politicalterrorscale.org.
   To compare the human rights records of states with representatives on these institutions, there is available a standard measure of human rights violations constructed by political scientists. It is a 5-point scale of human rights violations, from 1, where violations such as killing, torture, or political imprisonment are rare or exceptional, through 3, which describes situations where there is "extensive political imprisonment" and "execution or other political murders and brutality may be common," to 5, where violations extend to the entire population.

[20] See Eric Cox, "State Interests and the Creation and Functioning of the United Nations Human Rights Council," *Journal of International Law and International Relations* 6, no. 1 (2010): 87–120 for a comparison of earlier years.

members of the Council and the average violations for states world-wide. Redesigning the institution has not had a marked impact on the human rights qualities of those selected to manage human rights protection on behalf of the international community. By this measure, the Council represents continuity, not reform, in comparison to its predecessor and in comparison to the human rights performance of the rest of the world. Institutional designers created bodies that track global human rights performance quite closely. Adherence to human rights principles does not distinguish selection to this body. The inference is that member states sought the symbolism of reform, but were not prepared to delegate to a substantially stronger commitment device.

6

Despite governments' promises to give up repression, individuals around the world get tortured. In 2016 *Amnesty International* reported that in Laguna Province in the Philippines, police officers decided on the torture technique to use by spinning a roulette wheel. In 2015 in Mexico, *Human Rights Watch* reported that officials used beatings, waterboarding, sexual torture, and electric shocks to extract confessions.[21] You are not safe from torture in Syria or Nigeria, nor are you necessarily safe as a suspect in the custody of the Black Watch in Iraq. All these countries are state parties to the Convention Against Torture and are obliged to report to its treaty body.

With a range of human rights treaties and the security forces and officials of 193 member states, managing its own monitoring is too costly for the United Nations, and in any case the member states would be unlikely to agree to increasing its capacity in this way. Human rights conventions and the Human Rights Council require state parties to submit self-reports periodically. Some states, often

---

[21] Amnesty International, *Amnesty International Report 2015–2016: The State of the World's Human Rights* (London: Amnesty International, 2016), p. 293; Human Rights Watch, *World Report* (2015). https://www.hrw.org/world-report/2015 (accessed April 18, 2016).

those with very poor human rights records, are many years overdue (in 2015, India was thirteen years overdue with its International Convention on Civil and Political Rights report, and Egypt was eleven years overdue with its report under the Convention Against Torture). After all, why blow the whistle on one's own bad performance?

Getting around self-reporting is relatively straightforward: either do not submit, or submit a dishonest account. Yet it is not the only form of monitoring that states face in this policy area. How do states get around unwelcome third-party monitoring? Third parties might be other states or civil society organizations such as Amnesty International. As a result of the enormous expansion of global civil society and the capability of third-party "fire alarm" monitoring, political scientists are encouraged about the prospect for successful delegation in international relations.[22]

The prospect dims with awareness that states in turn adapt to the pressure from civil society. There is evidence that the increased flow of information about human rights conditions resulting from the mobilization of civil society has positive consequences on the delivery of human rights, and probably environmental protection, and other global public goods. While ratification of treaties may not make much difference in itself, when civil society mobilizes to inform international agencies and other members of the collective principal about human rights conditions in a particular state, and as a consequence puts pressure on a state to keep its treaty commitments, then compliance may improve.[23] But optimism about the expansion

[22] David Lake and Matthew McCubbins, "The Logic of Delegation to International Organizations," in Hawkins et al. (2006).

[23] For human rights see, for example, Christopher Fariss, "Respect for Human Rights Has Improved over Time: Modeling the Changing Standard of Accountability," *American Political Science Review* 108, no. 2 (2014): 297–318; Thomas Risse, Stephen C. Ropp, and Kathryn Sikkink, eds., *The Power of Human Rights* (Cambridge: Cambridge University Press, 1999); James Meernik et al., "The Impact of Human Rights Organizations on Naming and Shaming," *Journal of Conflict Resolution* 56, no. 2 (2012): 233–256; Matthew M. Krain, "J'accuse! Does Naming and Shaming Perpetrators Reduce the Severity of Genocides or Politicides?" *International Studies Quarterly* 56, no. 3 (2012): 574–589; Todd Landman, *Protecting Human Rights* (Washington, DC: Georgetown University Press, 2005); Beth Simmons, *Mobilizing for Human Rights* (Cambridge: Cambridge University Press, 2009); Alyson Brysk, *Speaking Rights to Power: Constructing Political Will* (Oxford: Oxford University Press, 2013).

of civil society and its effect on information asymmetries must be tempered by a concern for the strategic nature of the relationship between governments and civil society and for the opportunism and adaptability of defaulting and backsliding governments in the struggle to gain the information advantage.

Understanding the value of third-party monitoring to public policy delivery developed with the application of principal-agent theory to public administration in the United States.[24] Civil society associations and interest groups supply useful information on policy performance at little cost to legislators. For instance, cyclist organizations monitor potholes and accident hotspots. These groups compensate for information asymmetry in the principal-agent relationship and allow those in charge to reassert control when transportation agencies underperform. Similarly, international and national nongovernmental organizations (NGOs) monitor the performance of security agencies and report back to the human rights institutions of the international community. Interest groups or NGOs like Amnesty International expose hidden action by repressive states. They give the collective principal the opportunity to assert control.

With the proliferation of national and international NGOs, the expectation is that this flow of third-party information will steadily improve human rights conditions around the world. But before we put too much confidence in civil society and third-party monitoring, let us remind ourselves of the primacy of information in the principal-agent relationship and of the interactive nature of this relationship. It follows that if we start from a position of assuming that there is a strong incentive to keep hidden action hidden and of strategic interaction among the relevant actors, then the improvement in human

---

[24] This section draws on a large collaborative project with colleagues Kristin Bakke and Dominic Perera at UCL and Hannah Smidt at the University of Zurich. See Kristin M. Bakke, Neil J. Mitchell, and Hannah M. Smidt, "When States Crack Down on Human Rights Defenders," *International Studies Quarterly* 64, no. 1 (March 2020): 85–96; Hannah M. Smidt, Dominic Perera, Neil J. Mitchell, and Kristin M. Bakke, "Silencing Their Critics: How Government Restrictions against Civil Society Affect International 'Naming and Shaming,'" *British Journal of Political Science* online (February 2020): 1–22; see also Jeffrey Banks and Barry Weingast, "The Political Control of Bureaucracies under Asymmetric Information," *American Journal of Political Science* 36, no. 2 (1992): 509–524.

rights conditions will be punctuated by reversals. The relationship between civil society and governments goes both ways. If third parties inform on a state that continues to use repression despite its commitment to do otherwise, then the state responds to restore the information advantage, distort the monitoring, and silence the third-party informant. In many parts of the world, governments are not hampered by a domestic constitution that constrains their ability to shut down civil society organizations. Fire alarms can be tampered with or disabled. States that want to continue to use repression have an incentive to restrict the monitoring capacity of third parties and so evade accountability to the international community.

On July 1, 2016, the Human Rights Council warned of this very response by states as it considered Resolution 32/31 on Civil Society Space (2016). This resolution recognized "the crucial importance of the active involvement of civil society . . . in promoting good governance, including through transparency and accountability." It emphasized first and foremost "that creating and maintaining a safe and enabling environment in which civil society can operate free from hindrance and insecurity assists States in fulfilling their existing international human rights obligations and commitments."[25] The resolution urged states to protect these organizations and their staff from threats and intimidation, legal proceedings, counterterrorism measures, and other means of interfering with civil society organizations' operation and activities. The vote provided a test for countries with something to hide from the international community. They would be unlikely to support this resolution.

Thirty-one countries voted in favor of the resolution, seven members of the council voted against this resolution (China, Congo, Cuba, Nigeria, Russian Federation, South Africa, and the Bolivarian Republic of Venezuela), and there were nine abstentions (Bolivia, Burundi, Ethiopia, Kenya, Kyrgyzstan, Qatar, Saudi Arabia, United Arab Emirates, and Vietnam). States that do not deliver human

---

[25] United Nations General Assembly, "Resolution Adopted by the Human Rights Council on 1 July 2016: Civil Society Space," Human Rights Council 32 Session, A/HRC/RES/32/31, July 20 2016. https://documents-dds-ny.un.org/doc/UNDOC/GEN/G16/160/85/PDF/G1616085.pdf?OpenElement.

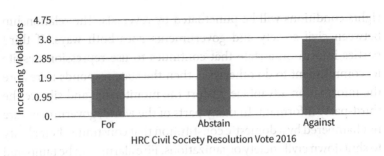

Figure 5.2. Support civil society? Not if you violate human rights.

rights protection have an incentive to weaken the commitment device, restrict civil society space, and interfere with the information flowing from civil society. They prefer to keep information about repressive activities private. Open civic space makes that harder. Figure 5.2 shows the average level of human rights violations[26] by vote choice for members of the Human Rights Council.

The voting pattern reflects the interactive relationship between civil society and states and fits expectations about who benefits from preserving information asymmetry. Human rights records progressively deteriorate as states move from supporting to abstaining to opposing this resolution. The votes of repressive states on this issue, unsurprisingly, suggest that they prefer to reduce the availability of third party fire alarm monitoring. Further analysis eliminating potential confounding factors is required, but the correlates of the vote fit theoretical expectations.

Third-party monitoring is key to successful delegation in the international sphere as principal-agent theory suggests, but in the real world we must anticipate the further adaptation of states and the consequent vulnerability of investigative reporters and civil society organizations and their staff around the world. To put the better angels of our nature in charge and improve the flow of relevant information, we need conditions that foster and protect, and do not

---

[26] Human rights violations are measured by the political terror scale from Gibney et al. (2015).

inhibit, the existence of civil society organizations. A key feature that distinguishes domestic American politics from the international sphere is the constitutional protections for freedom of association and speech. The standard principal-agent applications to politics and public administration, which were developed in the American context, have not been pushed in the direction of thinking about how those exposed by noisy fire alarm monitoring might react, other than with improved performance.

7

Finally, to return to the relationship between the United States and the Human Rights Council, in 2018, the Trump administration claimed the Human Rights Council was shirking its human rights task. Announcing the withdrawal of the United States, the US ambassador to the United Nations, Nikki Haley, was unequivocal about the weakness of this commitment device. She described the Human Rights Council as a "cesspool of political bias," preoccupied with Israeli violations, while "the world's most inhumane regimes continue to escape its scrutiny."[27] Clearly, it is by design a flawed commitment device, some of its members are shameless, and its performance is bound to be mixed at best. But without members of the collective principal retaining some control of the selection of agents, it is difficult to imagine states consenting to the delegation in the first place. If the only feasible alternative is not delegating, then we are better off with it than without it.

For the record, eleven other countries in addition to Israel were subject to specific scrutiny by the Council in 2018. They were Belarus, Cambodia, Central African Republic, North Korea, Eritrea, Iran, Mali, Myanmar, Somalia, Sudan, and Syria. On the face of it, these countries likely deserve scrutiny. Reacting to the US withdrawal,

---

[27] "US Quits UN Human Rights Council," *The Guardian*, June 19, 2018. https://www.theguardian.com/world/2018/jun/19/us-quits-un-human-rights-council-cesspool-political-bias.

Human Rights Watch pointed out that in its September 2018 session, the Council had created a unit to investigate abuses against the Rohinga in Myanmar, it had adopted the United Nations' first-ever resolution on the crisis in Venezuela, it had renewed the mandate of the UN investigation into abuses by all parties to the conflict in Yemen, and it had initiated a public discussion of a UN report on the treatment of human rights defenders in China, Egypt, and Bahrain, among others. These actions are consistent with the protection of human rights.

Individually and collectively, we struggle with inconsistent preferences, whether self-imposed or imposed on us by others. One common device to fix this self-control problem is to delegate. The drunk gives someone else the keys, or states give international agencies a whip to keep them or future governments to their human rights promises. But having made the decision to delegate, it does not mean that when the commitment starts to bite, whether with central bankers or with human rights agencies, actors will not try to browbeat, misinform, or even terminate the commitment-keeping agent.

6
Blame

The opportunism of the agent and what to do about it preoccupies principal-agent theorists. The theory's central concepts point to the agent's information advantage over the principal and his rational, self-interested, and perhaps perfidious behavior. As Tolstoy's Levin discovered with his farm laborers, their interests were flatly opposed to his. They mistreated the equipment and worked merrily. Agents betray the principal's trust. Yet principals also behave badly. And for them as well, delegation provides a mechanism to evade the consequences of their wrongdoing. The principal may use an agent in ways often not anticipated by the agent when he took on the task. He may not have agreed to carry the blame and is shocked to find himself in that position, but if a controversial action is exposed, the agent may find himself multitasking as a "fall guy." The most dramatic of the incentives actuating the delegation relationship is to evade blame and accountability for unworthy actions. It is a strong incentive. In the moment of the crisis, choosing whether or not to find someone else to blame for the wrongdoing is a litmus test for leaders. In that moment, few find the grace not to delegate this task. They will prefer to not carry the blame themselves.

With difficult policy choices, decision-makers may simply abdicate decision-making. Something may be in the national interest, but the potential cost for decision-makers is too high. An example is the closing of military bases by legislators in the United States. These bases are of great economic value and political consequence in the locations in which they are found. Closing them is difficult. When this policy issue needed addressing, Congress delegated responsibility for the policy to an agency. It provided insulation for those

Why Delegate?. Neil J. Mitchell, Oxford University Press (2021). © Oxford University Press.
DOI: 10.1093/oso/9780190904197.003.0006

politicians whose constituents had their base closed.[1] The redistribution of responsibility to the special agency was agreed up front; the agency knew it would take the blame or would get the credit, should it come to that. But sometimes the agent does not know what role he will assume when things go wrong.

The initial incentive to delegate may be some efficiency gain. Then, when things go wrong, the principal extracts an additional benefit from the agent in the effort to safeguard her power and position. She uses him to carry the blame. This political benefit to the principal may not be part of the initial agreement. Carrying the blame was not a task that the agent knew he would be undertaking; it may not even have been a benefit that the principal had anticipated. In the moment, the principal takes advantage of the delegation relationship, but outside any contractual agreement, in order to safeguard herself, at the expense of the agent.

1

In the event of scandal, self-interested individuals seek to evade responsibility and blame. They do not want punishment or unpleasant reputational, financial, legal, or personal consequences. The division of labor through delegation allows principals to separate themselves from what went wrong. Caught by surprise when a whistle-blower sounds the alarm, the principal sees a way out through the delegation relationship. As we know, contracts are difficult to draft and are incomplete, and contingencies arise. When contingencies arise, the question becomes who decides what happens.[2] The principal, higher on the chain of delegation, is best placed to say who is in the wrong, or to blame someone. After all, "fall guys" are usually not found

---

[1] See Morris Fiorina, "Legislative Choice of Regulatory Forms: Legal Process or Adminstrative Process?," *Public Choice* 39, no. 1 (1982): 33–66; Kenneth Mayer, Closing Military Bases (Finally): "Solving Collective Dilemmas Through Delegation," *Legislative Studies Quarterly* 20, no. 3 (1995): 393–413. An earlier version of this argument was developed in Mitchell, *Democracy's Blameless Leaders* (2012).

[2] Oliver Hart, "Incomplete Contracts and Control," *American Economic Review* 107, no. 7 (2017): 1731–1752.

higher on the chain of delegation. The principal's chief obstacle to control is knowing the agent's goals and what the agent is doing. With the attribution of blame, this lack of knowledge is a benefit. She takes advantage of the principal's proverbial disadvantage: information asymmetry. Under some conditions there may be value in at least appearing to know less rather than more. To keep up this appearance, leaders of large organizations may announce some sort of inquiry to find out what agents had been up to on their watch. The distance provided by delegation buffers the principal from negative external consequences of various sorts. Perhaps more worryingly, there is some evidence that it also buffers her from negative internal consequences and an uneasy conscience. Delegation allows one not to blame oneself. Whether the distribution of blame is the initial motivation for a delegation relationship, or if it only comes up after entering the relationship, an incentive to delegate is to shift the blame and evade accountability in whatever form that accountability might take, be it legal penalties and loss of liberty, financial losses, reputational losses, or a loss of sleep (not to be underestimated—as Macbeth found out).

2

How does this incentive show itself in practice? Leaders have probably always used delegation to protect power and position. Indeed, they have long been advised to do so. The technique is described in Machiavelli's *The Prince*. After violently subduing his opponents, Cesare Borgia shifted the blame for his cruelty to his Spanish minister, whose corpse was displayed in the town square in order to win over the public. Like the Saudi crown prince, the principal adds the role of "rogue" to the agent's duties; it is a service the agent performs, but one that he may not have known about or anticipated beforehand. In this version of the relationship, information asymmetry has reversed direction. It is the agent who suffers a lack of information about both the task to be undertaken and the character of the principal.

Even in the cradle of the theory of delegation, the firm, the incentives, and the locus for opportunism in this relationship should not be conceived as one-sided. While court proceedings are underway as I write, and while managers deny responsibility, recent management decisions at Volkswagen (VW) fit this part of the theoretical argument. It was not Spanish ministers, but software engineers who were put in the public square.

From Watergate to Dieselgate, you delegate if you do not want the blame. Dieselgate, VW's worldwide campaign to foil environmental regulations, saw managers hurriedly pointing the finger at the excesses of runaway software engineers. The software, if not the managers, knew how to cheat when a VW, or an Audi, or a Porsche was undergoing emissions testing. Under these conditions, the "defeat device" engaged the pollution controls on the vehicles. On the road again, and in order to improve fuel economy and acceleration, the vehicles pumped out up to thirty-five times more respiratory disease–causing nitrogen oxide. They created a mephitic scandal in the process.

There is a supervisory board at VW. Its monitoring did not get in the way of VW managers cheating environmental regulations. In discussing the role of boards, Fama and Jensen note that some corporations are dominated by an individual manager, which "in some cases signals the absence of separation of decision management and decision control [monitoring], and, in our theory, the organization suffers in the competition for survival."[3] Dieselgate was a survival-sized scandal, but VW's board was no match for vaulting managerial ambition to leap over all regulatory obstacles on the path to becoming the world's biggest car company. According to the financial press, VW had an authoritarian culture. The supervisory board had only one clearly independent outsider, with many of the others connected to the Piech and Porsche families. Ferdinand Piech (a grandson of Ferdinand Porsche, who founded Porsche and designed the VW Beetle) was a former CEO of VW and then was

---

[3] Fama and Jensen (1983), p. 314.

chair of the supervisory board until 2015. His wife was also on the board.[4] When the scandal was exposed, it was the non-family shareholders who roused themselves and took the corporation to court.

A third-party environmental group, which eventually caught up with VW and its emissions on a California road, had sounded the alarm. The company had cheated customers and the public for a decade. With the devices exposed, managers had questions to answer. The crisis arrived for the head of Volkswagen Group of America, Michael Horn, in the autumn of 2015. Congress administered his leadership litmus test. He chose to delegate the blame. He claimed that responsibility for the deception did not lie with the company. Designing and installing a defeat device was not VW's decision: "the investigations are ongoing, but this was not a corporate decision. . . . To my best knowledge today, the corporation in no Board meeting or no Supervisory Board meeting has authorized this, but this was a couple of software engineers who put this in, for whatever reasons. And I would also like to find out."[5] The man at the very top, VW CEO Martin Winterkorn, was similarly surprised at what was in the company's cars, and he wanted to get to the truth. The word from Wolfsburg, Germany, on September 23, 2015, was as follows:

> I am shocked by the events of the past few days. Above all, I am stunned that misconduct on such a scale was possible in the Volkswagen Group. As CEO I accept responsibility for the irregularities that have been found in diesel engines and have therefore requested the Supervisory Board to agree on terminating my function as CEO of the Volkswagen Group. I am doing this in the interests of the company even though I am not aware of any wrong doing on my part. . . . The process of clarification and transparency must continue. This is the only way to win back trust. I am

---

[4] "Boardroom Politics at the Heart of the VW Scandal," *The Financial Times*, October 4, 2015. https://www.ft.com/content/e816cf86-6815-11e5-a57f-21b88f7d973f.

[5] Testimony of Michael Horn, president and CEO of Volkswagen Group of America, Inc., before United States House Committee on Energy and Commerce, Subcommittee on Oversight and Investigations, October 8, 2015, 59.

convinced that the Volkswagen Group and its team will overcome this grave crisis.[6]

This is the classic, "responsibility-taking" formulation of the man at the top, reminiscent of Richard Nixon's resignation after Watergate. Notional responsibility is with the office, not the individual, who is shocked at the scale of misconduct by his subordinates. Dr. Winterkorn says he is the man at the top, but not the man in the wrong. Blame lies elsewhere. Ultimately, it will be an opportunity for an affirmative experience for the organization.

Winterkorn's statement elicited skepticism. Although "stunned" in September 2015, in 2014 his company had been notified of its failure to deliver on its environmental claims. Defeat devices could be found in its cars from at least 2006. The device was part of a "science-based" public relations campaign that began around the same time. The campaign was initiated to counter efforts to regulate diesel cars and to prepare the way for VW management's aim to expand market share in the United States. Journalists Geoffrey Smith and Roger Parloff, in a piece entitled "Hoaxwagen," noted that Audi engineers arrived at the same solution for "clean" diesel in a separate location from the "first group of purported bad-apple engineers. That means two groups of engineers were allegedly breaking the law in parallel for seven years, with seemingly little in common except the upper-level executives they answered to."[7] In January 2018, *New York Times* reporter Jake Ewing revealed that VW used the fake emissions data for some sponsored experimental research.[8] In 2014, in a laboratory in Albuquerque, New Mexico, the European Research Group on Environment and Health in the Transport Sector, a group that represented VW, BMW, and Daimler, funded an experiment in which monkeys inhaled fumes from a VW Beetle

---

[6] Resignation statement by Dr. Winterkorn, September 22, 2015. Available at https://www.volkswagen-newsroom.com/en/press-releases/statement-by-prof-dr-winterkorn-1987.

[7] Geoffrey Smith and Roger Parloff, "Hoaxwagen," *Fortune*, March 7, 2016, p. 114.

[8] "10 Monkeys and a Beetle: Inside VW's Campaign for 'Clean Diesel,'" *New York Times*, January 30, 2018. https://www.nytimes.com/2018/01/25/world/europe/volkswagen-diesel-emissions-monkeys.html?searchResultPosition=2.

equipped with the defeat device, while watching cartoons on television (cartoons lower monkey stress). Researchers experimented on human subjects in Aachen, Germany. Delegating to this research group did allow the car companies to claim some distance and deniability. On exposure, they "repudiated the work of the group." But as Ewing points out, they had representatives on the group's board and came up with all the funding. After the story broke, the new VW CEO, Mattias Mueller, claimed, like his predecessor, to be stunned. He suspended a lobbyist and said the company would investigate. Ewing's *New York Times* stories drew comparisons with the tobacco industry sponsoring research to influence regulation of its harmful products, and noted that in 2012, the World Health Organization classified diesel emissions as a carcinogen. A German commentator on corporate governance said that VW was "playing the game where the subordinates were the culprits."[9] Subordinates may, of course, be culprits. If they had the approval of top managers, it implicates the principal; it does not exonerate them. The designers of the device that VW installed would have known they were doing wrong, but presumably were not expecting all the blame. The scapegoat analogy is not necessarily accurate for this type of delegation relationship. That goat *was* innocent. It was driven off with the sins of others.

Another recurring feature illustrated by this case was that the cheating chip was not found by regulatory agencies. It was a third-party fire alarm environmental group, the International Council on Clean Transportation (ICCT), that exposed the chicanery. John German and Peter Mock of ICCT observed that diesel cars appeared to perform to higher environmental standards in the United States than they did elsewhere. They thought that the evidence from road testing VWs in the United States would provide a way of ratcheting up environmental performance in Europe. The results of the test surprised the researchers. It revealed emissions at levels much higher than the company claimed. The ICCT sounded the alarm. It shared

9 "Volkswagen Suspends Top Lobbyist Amid Inquiry into Diesel Tests on Monkeys," *New York Times*, January 30, 2018. https://www.nytimes.com/2018/01/30/business/energy-environment/german-carmakers-diesel-monkeys.html.

its findings with VW, the Environmental Protection Agency, and the California Air Resources Board. VW did not want to hear, but an active civil society alerted bureaucrats and legislators to the problem and protected the respiration of the rest of us.

After their cheating was exposed, and although they knew what had happened, to back up their claim of information asymmetry VW hired an American law firm to carry out an independent inquiry into what they had been doing. Inquiries buy time and suggest a good faith effort on the part of those in charge to get to the bottom of a scandal. As the inquiry proceeds, public curiosity may dissipate, overtaken by other events. Notwithstanding VW's initial commitment to transparency, when the inquiry report was ready, the company refused to release it.

The scale of the financial and reputational disaster for VW supplied a strong incentive for shareholders to become active. At least it did for the minority of "non-familial" shareholders. VW's largest shareholders, along with the Piech and Porsche families, are Qatar and the State of Lower Saxony. In November 2017, the group of minority shareholders asked the court to appoint an independent expert to investigate the role of VW's top management in the scandal. Despite Dr. Winterkorn's pledge of transparency, the company fought this investigation to the highest court in Germany. VW lost there, too.

VW survives, but suffers from the debacle. Agency loss in the chain of delegation, somewhere between the shareholders and two rogue software engineers, amounts to $30 billion and counting, with class action suits to settle, criminal proceedings and cars to fix. What reportedly drove managers at VW was a strategic goal to increase market share in the United States, where it underperformed. The managers wanted to run the largest car company in the world. Four years after his resignation, Dr. Winterkorn faces criminal fraud charges in Germany. German prosecutors date his knowledge of the defeat device to 2006, not 2015 as he had claimed.

When things go wrong and when denial and delay do not seem to be working, principals resort to delegation. The information asymmetry that customarily accompanies delegation gives denial plausibility. But in this case, there is not a conventional principal–agent problem. There was no genuine information asymmetry affecting the principal.

At the extreme, and despite the Machiavellian tendencies of those in authority and how they later depict organizational relationships, activity that might as a consequence bring into question the survival of the decision-maker or the organization is likely to be controlled more closely. And if there is some delegation, the discretion of the agent will be limited and is indeed self-limiting. If we think again of the boundaries of delegation and how tasks get distributed in the real world, there are circumstances under which risk-averse agents will themselves want to limit their autonomy and not engage in "hidden action." Whatever the principals later say, agents are unlikely to independently and systematically engage the organization in illegal or reckless survival-threatening activity without covering themselves. They will seek some form of at least tacit approval from the principal. It would have been remarkable for the software engineers to take the initiative and decide on misconduct on this scale on their own. They would be unlikely to want sole responsibility for cheating, although when the scandal was exposed that was what the leadership team at VW required of them. As Jack Ewing reported, the "rogue" VW engineers had sought approval from top management.[10] The engineers presumably did so because they knew they were deceiving consumers and the nitrous oxide–breathing public and were doing wrong.

3

Eric Fair was a contract interrogator with US forces at Abu Ghraib and in Falluja who knew he did wrong. His memoir, *Consequence*, movingly describes the shame of his experience, his personal

---

[10] "VW Engineers Wanted O.K. from the Top for Emissions Fraud, Documents Show," *New York Times*, May 17, 2017. https://www.nytimes.com/2017/05/17/business/volkswagen-muller-diesel-emissions.html.

accountability, and his later struggle to put things as right as he could. Prior to Iraq, he had served as a paratrooper with the 101st Airborne and as a police officer in Bethlehem, Pennsylvania. With the invasion of Iraq, he signed up with CACI International, a private contractor used by the Pentagon. Aiding his selection, he had Arab-language training and in the army he had been through its very tough Survival, Evasion, Resistance, and Escape (SERE) program. This program simulated the treatment that might be given American prisoners of war and it then informed the torture regime that was developed by US forces and used at Abu Ghraib.

CACI International was not a well-run firm, by Fair's account. While his experience and training recommended him, the firm recruited haphazardly. It did not provide adequate preparation for interrogators. At Abu Ghraib early in 2004, Fair describes the escalating insurgency, the poor support, and the pressure on interrogators to extract more information. He did not work in the area of Abu Ghraib where the worst of the abuse occurred and which was later to appear in photographs, but Fair thought that what went on in the detention centers and prisons in Iraq was approved. While at Abu Ghraib he was interviewed by the Army Criminal Investigation Division about detainee abuse. At that time, he refused to check "the appropriate box" to indicate knowledge of wrongdoing. In April 2004, he saw the CBS 60 Minutes broadcast on Abu Ghraib: "Some of the activities in the photographs are familiar to me. Others are not. But I am not shocked. Neither is anyone else who served at Abu Ghraib. Instead, we are shocked by the performance of the men who stand behind microphones and say things like 'bad apples' and 'Animal House on night shift.'"[11] Fair was shocked to find out that those who served were out of control and acting in conflict with the principal's goals. Fair's contract did not include being the "fall guy." Taking the blame for abuse at Abu Ghraib was not what he had anticipated when agreeing to go to Iraq.

In 2017 in New York, I had the chance to speak with Eric Fair. His memoir makes clear how troubled he was by the situation he found

[11] Eric Fair, Consequence (New York: Henry Holt, 2016), p. 119.

himself in and by his own behavior. But those involved in the abuse, he said, were given no reason to believe they were doing anything unauthorized by those in charge: "it wasn't as if they were doing these things hoping not to get caught." Some years after returning from Iraq, in his effort to come to grips with what he had seen and done, he wrote a column for the *Washington Post* describing the abuses in Iraq. It attracted hate messages and the interest of the Department of Justice. They asked again why he had not checked the appropriate box in the earlier investigation in 2004. He said "I'm not proud of that."[12] This time he detailed what went on, but he was not prosecuted. I asked him why he had not checked the box when interviewed at Abu Ghraib. He said that "there was a bond of loyalty to fellow soldiers, which should be hard to break," and that he thought he was working for "an organization on the right side." Fair did not see what was going on at Abu Ghraib as agents acting opportunistically. But the whistle-blower, Joseph Darby, "made it impossible to ignore," he said, and the leadership "had to investigate themselves in some ways." Fair's account is compelling. He came forward voluntarily and was willing to face the consequences. The agents had no idea they had gone rogue, which "is not to say soldiers didn't deserve to get punished," Fair told me.

When the scandal was exposed, the interrogators and guards were burdened with the blame by their superiors. They thought they were using techniques authorized by those in charge. The leadership's goal was to gain intelligence information about a gathering insurgency. The invasion of Iraq was not going as anticipated. Lawyers for the administration had provided legal authority for "enhanced interrogation techniques" in what later were known as the "torture memos." On one memo about enhanced techniques and stress positions, Secretary of Defense Donald Rumsfeld famously had queried why standing was only for four hours, noting that he stood for eight to ten hours a day. When the CBS television program broadcast the pictures of the application of these techniques, perhaps he simply lacked the imaginative capacity to visualize what he had authorized.

---

[12] Ibid., p. 104.

Eleven years before Martin Winterkorn, Rumsfeld followed the standard man-at-the-top routine. When the crisis arrived, his leadership litmus test was administered by the Senate Armed Services Committee in May 2004. He testified:

> Mr. Chairman, members of the committee, in recent days there has been a good deal of discussion about who bears responsibility for the terrible activities that took place at Abu Ghraib. These events occurred on my watch. As secretary of defense, I am accountable for them and I take full responsibility. It's my obligation to evaluate what happened, to make sure that those who have committed wrong-doing are brought to justice, and to make changes as needed to see that it doesn't happen again.

In Rumsfeld's understanding, "full responsibility" entailed finding out what happened and bringing the actual wrongdoers to justice. It is not responsibility for the wrongdoing. He had the opportunity to shoulder some of the burden for the wrongdoing. He wanted none of it. He continued his testimony: "I can't conceive of anyone looking at the pictures and suggesting anyone could have recommended, condoned, permitted, encouraged, subtly, directly, in any way, that those things take place." The Senate Armed Services Committee's inquiry released five years later did conceive of Abu Ghraib in a way that Rumsfeld could not. Its report concluded that "the abuse of detainees at Abu Ghraib was not simply the result of a few soldiers acting on their own. . . . Secretary of Defense Donald Rumsfeld's December 2, 2002 authorization of aggressive interrogation techniques and subsequent interrogation policies and plans approved by senior military and civilian officials conveyed the message that physical pressures and degradation were appropriate treatment for detainees in U.S. military custody. What followed was an erosion in standards dictating that detainees be treated humanely."[13] The soldiers knew they had the task of interrogation enhanced by

---

[13] Committee on Armed Services, United States Senate, *Inquiry into the Treatment of Detainees in U.S. Custody* (November 20, 2008): p. xxix; "Rumsfeld Speaks Before the Senate Armed Services Committee on Abuse in Iraqi Prison," *CNN Transcripts* (May 7, 2004). http://transcripts.cnn.com/TRANSCRIPTS/0405/07/se.01.html.

degradation and abuse, but not the blame. Although Rumsfeld depicted it as a simple principal–agent problem, as Eric Fair said, it was not as if they were hoping to avoid getting caught. It was not action they were hiding from the principal.

In related research on intelligence sharing by British intelligence personnel and collusion in torture, political scientists Ruth Blakeley and Sam Raphael describe officials anxious to limit their own discretion and seeking specific authorization from the government. One source testified: "why should my officers carry the risks on behalf of the government personally?"[14] But at Abu Ghraib, it was those at the bottom of the chain of command who personally had to carry the convictions and prison time. Just as cautious principals prepare for agent opportunism and develop a sequence of responses to correct for it, perhaps they, like the software engineers, should have anticipated how the principal would react in a crisis—the capacity for opportunism and willingness to deny knowledge of the wrongdoing.

4

The blame incentive for delegation may form after entering into the relationship with an agent. Or sometimes it is there from the outset. Sometimes the principal knows the agent will seek some private benefit, but in doing so will contribute to her goals. She prospectively designs delegation with the attribution of blame in mind, rather than responding to some unforeseen contingency. Those in charge know the character and motivations of the agents they are recruiting, they know what these agents are likely to do if they have the chance, and they decide to look away. They willfully ignore the agent's actions as long as they derive some benefit from the delegation relationship. This scenario suggests a principal who *won't control*, not one who

---

[14] Ruth Blakeley and Sam Raphael, "Accountability, Denial and the Future-Proofing of British Torture," *International Affairs* 96, no. 3 (2020): 707. .

can't control.[15] The success of this blame-management strategy rests on the acceptance that the principal had a simple principal–agent problem. It follows that the principal needs to be able to claim information asymmetry and to be able to show that the agent derived a separate and private benefit from the task.

Won't *control* is not agency loss and at the expense of the principal, as the agent is contributing to the achievement of the principal's goal. Instead, it is a welcome loss of responsibility. Genuine information asymmetry impedes the principal's ability to control the agent. But there are also cases of the principal's *artificial* information asymmetry, where those in charge enter the relationship with the necessary information about the character of the agent. She knows what the agent is likely to do with the authority given to him. In this situation, principals do not lose control. They refuse control for as long as it is in their interest to do so.

Under the standard assumption of goal conflict between principal and agent, refusing control gives agents the opportunity to pursue private goals that are flatly opposed to those of the principal, like Levin's laborers. But the claim that the agent's private gain is the principal's loss simply does not always hold in the real world. Goal conflict is too readily assumed, and it may lead to the error of absolving the principal when in fact she is responsible. A more realistic theory of delegation must recognize that while the goals of the principal and the agent may be different, they are not necessarily in conflict. The agent can be narrowly selfish and singularly motivated by very private benefits, but these benefits may not conflict with the principal's strategic objective. The private benefit sought by the agent may contribute to the organizational or strategic goal sought by the principal.

If we think about delegation in warfare and implementing a type of violence that is widely condemned (for example, sexual violence) or choosing a target that is supposed to be off limits (for example,

---

[15] For early versions of this part of the argument, see Mitchell, *Agents of Atrocity* (2004), which used evidence from the English Civil War, the Russian Civil War, and the Israel-Palestine conflict, and Mitchell, Carey, and Butler (2014) for global data on militias and violations.

violence aimed at the civilian population), principals may look to use non-state agents in addition to their regular forces. They outsource some controversial and fear-inspiring violence to militias, local war lords, vigilantes, or death squads outside the direct chain of command. In addition to the logistical incentives of quickly multiplying forces or recruiting some local cultural expertise, evading blame is one universal and enduring political incentive that helps explain the persistence of these irregular groups and militias.

We have a fictionalized account of the good and the evil done by the irregulars who sided with the British and the French in the French and Indian War of 1756–1763 (the Seven Years' War). Colonel George Monro's daughters, Alice and Cora, have a regular soldier, Major Heyward, as an escort, but can we forget the bravery and skill of Chingachgook, Uncas, and Hawkeye? More darkly, can we forget Magua? In *The Last of the Mohicans*, James Fenimore Cooper describes the final days of one irregular band, if not the end of these sorts of groups. These informal armed groups perform well in fiction and on film, whether they are Bedouins bringing down the Ottoman Empire in *Lawrence of Arabia*, the American volunteer fighting against Franco in *For Whom the Bell Tolls*, or one colonial and two Native Americans defending the innocent in *The Last of the Mohicans*. We have an ineffable attachment to volunteers and adventurers who operate alongside the police or the army, but these agents often act less selflessly in practice. In other words, we should expect Magua and the Hurons, rather than Hawkeye and the Mohicans, to be the rule.

In 1757, in Fenimore Cooper's fictionalized account, an outpost north of New York City fell to French siege and Magua's Huron warriors:

> The cruel work was still unchecked. On every side the captured were flying before their relentless persecutors, while the armed columns of the Christian King stood fast, in an apathy which has never been explained.[16]

---

[16] James Fenimore Cooper, *The Last of the Mohicans* (New York: Penguin Books, [1826] 1986), p. 179.

Actually, the author does proffer an explanation for the "apathy" of the regular forces of the "Christian King" and what happened at Fort William Henry. Before the mayhem, Magua spoke for the informal group of agents to whom violence was delegated. He specified the private benefits they expected from the relationship with the French general: "not a warrior has a scalp, and the pale faces make friends!"[17] The general, who suffered mortal wounds on Quebec's Plains of Abraham two years later, is a Machiavellian, ends-and-means calculating, if regretful principal: "Montcalm, who felt that his influence over the warlike tribes he had gathered, was to be maintained by concession, rather than by power . . . became keenly sensible of the deep responsibility they assume, who disregard the means to attain their end, and of all the danger of setting in motion an engine, which it exceeds human power to control."[18] On the first day of the siege, according to historian Ian Steele, Montcalm called on Monro to surrender. He declared, "I have it yet in my power to restrain the savages, and oblige them to observe a capitulation, as hitherto none of them has been killed, which will not be in my power in other circumstances."[19] At Fort William Henry, those who give the orders and those who carried them out have different, but not conflicting, goals. In this case the principal has the strategic goal of taking a fort, and the agent has the separate and private goal of taking a scalp in Fennimore Cooper's story. The agent's private goal has instrumental value for the principal. It lowers the need for other incentives. In fact, Montcalm specifically asserts that the agents' private incentive is so powerful and independent of his and the mission's motivation that the agents, once loose, cannot be controlled. The assertion may be a bargaining ploy to frighten the defenders into submission, as well as an announcement that he will not be accountable for what happens next. Either the threat or the reality of these runaway agents seeking their private goods also promises to deliver the strategic goal.

[17] Ibid., p. 169.
[18] Ibid., pp. 170–171.
[19] Ian K. Steele, *Betrayals: Fort William Henry and the "Massacre"* (New York: Oxford University Press, 1990), p. 99.

5

The incentive to use but not to be responsible for excessive violence tempts political leaders into dangerous relationships with armed groups. They plead "vain command," saying that the warriors are beyond their power to control, and so relieve themselves of responsibility and delegate the blame. This incentive motivates leaders from whom we might expect better. I am not thinking of Christian Kings, but leaders in established democracies pledged to the rule of law and accountable to an electorate.

In 1921, the Anglo-Irish Treaty established the Irish Free State, leaving Northern Ireland as part of the United Kingdom. Among the articles in this treaty are those making financial provisions for the members of the security forces, given the change of government. The treaty stipulated that the "Irish Free State agrees to pay fair compensation . . . to . . . members of Police Forces and other Public Servants who are discharged by it or who retire in consequence of the change of government. . . . *Provided that this agreement shall not apply to members of the Auxiliary Police Force or to persons recruited in Great Britain for the Royal Irish Constabulary* [my italics]."[20] The treaty denied compensation to the British government's irregular forces, the members of the Auxiliary forces, and other British recruits. These were individuals who had responded to the British government's call to arms and its makeshift arrangements to muster recruits to suppress an increasingly bloody insurgency with brutal means. They were left out of the postwar contract.

The fighting between British forces and Irish Republicans began in January 1919, when the Irish Republican Army (IRA) killed two members of the Royal Irish Constabulary (RIC). With the loss of life and with the support for the Republican cause, the RIC had difficulty recruiting in Ireland. The British government supplemented the regular security forces with ex-soldiers from Britain, both

---

[20] Anglo-Irish Treaty, December 6, 1921. Available at http://treaty.nationalarchives.ie/document-gallery/anglo-irish-treaty-6-december-1921/; see also Fedorowich, "The Problems of Disbandment: The Royal Irish Constabulary and Imperial Migration, 1919–1929," *Irish Historical Studies* 30, no. 117 (1996): 88–110.

as special recruits within the RIC and as a separate auxiliary militia. Newspapers carried advertisements for service in what was called "the Corps d'Élite." Those interested were invited to join the Auxiliary Division of the Royal Irish Constabulary.[21] The general commanding this corps wrote a letter to the *Times* describing the "unique" force and urging former officers to enlist in order to "overthrow the gang of assassins who call themselves the Irish Republican Army."[22] A separate group of recruits were dubbed the "Black and Tans," after their distinctive uniforms and a famous pack of hunting dogs.[23] They were ex-soldiers and under the command of the RIC. The Auxiliary Division was a separate force.

Both organizations quickly gained notoriety for the way they carried out their task. At a cabinet meeting chaired by Prime Minister David Lloyd George, the RIC commander reported drunkenness in the Auxiliaries and described the reprisals carried out by this force, which had included arson in the city of Cork.[24] Elsewhere they shot prisoners and looted shops.[25] The *Times* took the position that "we have long known that the Auxiliary Division was designed for a purpose which we have regarded as foolish and immoral, and that very nature of its employment renders discipline in its ranks almost impossible."[26] The newspaper suggests that the Auxiliary Division's immoral conduct and "control problems" were part of the contract.

The risk to civilians was brought to the government's attention by the leading newspaper of the day and even more directly. In March 1921, the Archbishop of Canterbury met the Lord Chancellor, Lord Birkenhead, who represented the government in the House of Lords on Irish issues. The Archbishop questioned the minister about the ill-discipline of the Auxiliaries. Lord Birkenhead conceded that "outrages have been committed by the Auxiliary Force," but it had been vital in controlling the situation.[27] The risk to civilians was one

---

21 " Join—The Corps d'élite," *Times*, November 2, 1920, p. 9.
22 "Recruiting for the R.I.C.," *Times*, December 14, 1920, p. 8.
23 Richard Bennett, *The Black and Tans* (Barnsley, UK: Pen and Sword Books, 2010).
24 The Cabinet Papers, CAB/23/30. UK National Archives, June 2, 1922.
25 See Bennett (2010), pp. 163–166.
26 Quoted in Bennett (2010), p. 174.
27 The Cabinet Papers, CAB/24/122. UK National Archives, March 21, 1921.

the government was willing to accept. Later assessments of the effectiveness of these forces concurred with the Lord Chancellor's. The strategy of using these forces and these methods did not defeat the insurgency; perhaps that had not been achievable, but it was instrumental in getting the Republicans to negotiate.[28]

The British government used the Auxiliaries and the Black and Tans to multitask. They needed boots on the ground. The regular forces' recruiting difficulties pointed to the need to find the numbers of personnel for the task. These types of forces also had the "foolish and immoral" task of imposing brutal repression, while saving the government's reputation. There is evidence that the government calculated that repressing the insurgents required harsher methods than could be officially condoned or that could be linked with the regular forces.[29] They sought to evade accountability for these methods. Like Montcalm's Huron warriors, these arms-length, makeshift organizations, with their own unstoppable motivations, distanced the government from the implementation of violence. There is a strategic rationality driving the use of these agents. They expanded the types of violence available to the government side, commensurate with the threat posed by a "gang of assassins," and without the damage to the institutions and reputations of the regular forces.

Not all were happy with outsourcing brutality or with this blame-evading incentive for delegation. The chief of the Imperial General Staff, no-nonsense Field Marshal Sir Henry Wilson, was against a policy of reprisals without official responsibility. His view was that if the government wished to murder people, it should do it itself. It should not shift responsibility to these other forces. Wilson's diary describes a meeting with the prime minister and other ministers on September 29, 1920:

---

[28] Bennett (2010), p. 220.

[29] The costs of the use of cruelty rather than lenity in Henry V's terms was again illustrated in Northern Ireland in the 1970s. Ian Cobain describes an informal survey of IRA prisoners indicating that 90 percent had joined that organization not for ideological reasons but in order to respond to security force use of torture, unlawful killing as at Bloody Sunday, and internment without trial. See Ian Cobain, *Anatomy of a Killing: Life and Death on A Divided Island* (London: Granta, 2020).

I told them what I thought of reprisals by the "Black and Tans," and how this must lead to chaos and ruin. . . . I pointed out that these reprisals were carried out without anyone being responsible; men were murdered, houses burnt, villages wrecked (such as Balbriggan, Ennistymon, Trim, etc.). I said that this was due to want of discipline, and this must be stopped. It was the business of Government to govern. If these men ought to be murdered, then the Government ought to murder them. . . . I am glad I am in no way responsible, and that I have protested for months against this method of out-terrorizing the terrorists by irresponsible persons.[30]

Here we have the top British military official pointing to a blame-management incentive to delegate the task to this improvised security organization made up of agents willing to commit reprisals. It was a group designed to out-terrorize the terrorists. The following month, Wilson had another talk with the prime minister. Lloyd George said that he would "shoulder the responsibility for reprisals, but wanted to wait till the American elections are over."[31] On November 6, Wilson complained, "more murders in Ireland yesterday, and more reprisals. How the Cabinet can agree to all this and not take the responsibility absolutely beats me, or how they think this class of work will solve the Irish question passes my comprehension."[32] Wilson was not alone in criticizing the use of these irregulars. The opposition Liberal Party leader pointed to the lethal apathy of the government. He argued that the reprisals could not be dismissed as the actions of ill-disciplined individuals or "bad apples." It was not a simple principal–agent problem: "If the Executive disapproves of these things, why does it not prevent them, and if it cannot prevent them why does it not punish them?"[33] Not using these terms, he suggests that the violations in Ireland were a case of *won't control*

[30] C. E. Callwell, *Field-Marshal Sir Henry Wilson: His Life and Diaries* (London: Cassell, 1927), pp. 263–264.

[31] Ibid., p. 265.

[32] Ibid., p. 268.

[33] House of Commons Debates, November 24, 1920, cc. 490–491. Available at https://www.theyworkforyou.com/debates/?id=1920-11-24a.490.0.

rather than *can't control*, as the agents were not punished in a timely and appropriate way for their actions. Wilson's diary provides direct testimony to the government's information and knowledge about what their agents were doing in Ireland. Leaders were not suffering information asymmetry. Yet they would not take control of these agents or disband them if they were beyond control.

As we have seen, armies have *can't control* problems like any other organization. Soldiers commit war crimes on their own behalf and without strategic benefits. Armies have simple principal–agent problems, which the hierarchy then cover up for fear of the agent confidence factor. The principal's guile is retrospective in aiding the agent in hiding or excusing his misconduct. With *won't control*, the guile is prospective. At times a government may recruit or select these agents, place them in position and anticipate their misconduct, expecting a strategic benefit from their actions. Leaders look away as long as the benefit is delivered.

Armament and communications have come a long way since the French and Indian War when North America was a wilderness. Political leadership has not. In addition to war-fighting efficiencies and loyalty, militias offer political savings for the government. The use of a militia may shift accountability for immoral and illegal acts. As the evidence suggests in Ireland, or in Russia's use of "Hell's Angels"–type groups in the Crimea, for example, non-state armed groups give some deniability to government leaders. We are not surprised to find these armed groups in weak states lacking the capacity to form professional security forces. We do not expect strong states like the Russian Federation to give guns and authority to two-wheeled "Night Wolves" in Sevastopol.[34] We think of violence as one of those special responsibilities, like justice or diplomacy, that belong to and ought to remain with the state. But delegating to this type of organization presents government leaders an opportunity to deliver violence and repression at lower reputational cost. In contrast

---

[34] "Putin's Angels: The Bikers Battling for Russia in Ukraine," *The Guardian*, January 29, 2016. https://www.theguardian.com/world/2016/jan/29/russian-biker-gang-in-ukraine-night-wolves-putin.

to the clearer chain of command linking leaders to regular forces, these irregulars are removed from the state. Commanders may not bother to control, if the violence delivers some strategic goal, or when the violence itself provides some incentive for the agents, as with a fictionalized warrior's demand for scalps, or rape instead of pay for South Sudan militias. A United Nations investigation of South Sudan in 2016 revealed widespread sexual violence. Commanders substituted rape for pay as the incentive for pro-government militiamen. On the roadside, in front of her children, a mother was stripped and raped by five soldiers.[35] The *can't control/won't control* dynamic is fundamental to the state's enduring relationship with irregular armed groups. But as Fenimore Cooper suggests with his comment about the "inexplicable" apathy of the Christian King, it is difficult to get dispositive evidence of *won't control*. That is its enduring attraction. But there are some signs to look for.

6

What sort of evidence might help distinguish *won't control*? A strength of principal-agent theory is that it provides clear and counterfactually useful expectations about the type of response one expects from a principal who is genuinely interested in controlling the opportunistic agent. As a consequence, it offers pointers about how a responsible rather than cynical principal is expected to behave in order to safeguard herself from agent opportunism. Screening, monitoring, and punishment are the means used to control agents. If some or all of these measures are absent, or only undertaken in a token way, then it suggests that the principal is at least indifferent to an agent's opportunism, if not positively benefiting from it.

For *won't control*, first there must be compatibility, rather than conflict, between the agent's selfishness and the principal's strategic

---

[35] "Pro-government Militias 'Told to Rape Women in Lieu of Pay' as War Crimes Continue in South Sudan," *Independent*, March 11, 2016. https://www.independent.co.uk/news/world/africa/pro-government-militias-told-rape-women-lieu-pay-war-crimes-continue-south-sudan-a6924956.html.

preferences. The principal's goals are key. There must be some identifiable strategic goal that is compatible with the agents' identifiable private goal. For example, there must be a plausible strategic narrative that fits with a refusal to control selfish, agent-centered violence and looting. Montcalm had the strategic goal of taking the fort. The British wanted to keep the United States on its side and get the Irish Republicans to the negotiating table. As for the measures a conventional principal is expected to take, an indicator of *won't control* might be found in the principal's selection and positioning of agents. Despite prior knowledge of the agents' character and some earlier performance which indicates the likelihood of abuse, the agent is selected and deployed. In *The Last of the Mohicans*, Montcalm knew the proclivities of his allies. Or prior to its use by the Israeli government in the 1982 invasion of Lebanon, the revenge-filled Christian Phalange militia in Lebanon had a known history of conflict with Palestinians and of being both a victim and perpetrator of massacres. A previous Israeli prime minister, Moshe Sharett, avoided entanglement with this group because of the risks they presented. Prime Minister Menachem Begin and Defense Minister Ariel Sharon were more willing to gamble. They deployed the Lebanese militia into the Palestinian refugee camps, where they committed a massacre. When this massacre provoked international outrage, Israeli leaders expressed shock and surprise and the militia were blamed.

Another indicator is that the abuse or "rogue behavior" is not isolated. It is part of a pattern. The rogue behavior involves a number of agents. Or it stretches across a period of time during which the principal had an opportunity to intervene, but did not. A lack of effort by the principal to monitor and call off the agents, when given information about their abuses, indicates *won't control*, as with the use of the Auxiliaries in Ireland when the government was alerted by newspapers, senior military commanders, and politicians. When the Christian Phalange were in the Beirut camps, reports of the ongoing slaughter from individual Israeli soldiers and journalists were not acted upon by the Israeli commanders and political leaders in a timely way. The "cruel work" of the revenge-seeking Lebanese

Christian militia was left unchecked for thirty-six hours by an "apathetic" Israeli army and its defense minister.

Finally, a lack of effort to correct or punish agents after the event suggests a *won't control* commander. With militias, at least, it is unlikely that punishment carries the same risks for the commander as it does with members of the regular forces. Punishing militias is unlikely to worry the regulars. All the same, conclusive evidence of *won't control* is problematic, and diary entries from the likes of plain-speaking Sir Henry Wilson are a rare find. The Israeli Kahan Commission of Inquiry into the massacre in the Palestinian refugee camps concluded it was *can't control*. They attributed the selection of these agents and the slow response to the incompetence of the Israeli authorities and a failure to put adequate monitoring and supervision structures in place.[36]

7

How effective is delegation in helping leaders avoid blame and punishment? It is a desperate measure and the results are mixed for the cases I have picked. It bought some time, but Martin Winterkorn has been charged with aggravated fraud by German prosecutors and is under indictment in the United States, only low-level personal served prison time for Abu Ghraib, and Sharon went on to become prime minister.

If delegation helps avoid punishment imposed by others, what of that which we may impose on ourselves? Sometimes our conscience catches up with us. Defense Minister Sharon claimed to be shocked by the militia's actions and told the Israeli Knesset that responsibility lay with the militia and not the Israeli Defense Force (IDF): "the hands of the I.D.F. are clean, purity of arms was preserved there too. . . . We did not imagine in our worst dreams that the Phalangists would act in this way when they entered the battle at this stage of the

---

[36] Kahan Commission, "The Beirut Massacre: The Complete Kahan Commission Report" (New York: Karz-Cohl, 1983).

fighting. . . . The inhuman tragedy which occurred was beyond our control. With all the pain and sorrow, we will not agree to shoulder it."[37] Sharon distanced his government, his regular forces, and himself from for the atrocity. The motivations of the militia were beyond his imagination and their actions were beyond his control. In contrast, in Fenimore Cooper's fictionalized account, Montcalm knew the cruel work Magua had in mind and, if the historical account is to be credited, Montcalm was at least personally aware of what he had set in motion.

There is some experimental evidence that delegation can provide psychological detachment and relieve any internal or personal feeling of accountability. Economists John Hamman, George Loewenstein, and Roberto Weber's research shows that delegation reduces the personal cost of a selfish or immoral action: "acting through agents allows principals to maintain positive impressions of their own behavior and role in determining outcomes. Agents serve this function through a subtle interplay of psychological factors. Principals do not feel that they are behaving unfairly because they do not directly take immoral actions; they simply hire agents."[38] In the experiment, subjects allocate money to a recipient either directly or through an agent. If the giving is direct, rather than through an agent, the recipient receives a more generous share. When the allocation is placed at arm's length, through an agent, subjects act more selfishly. Agents were also free to decide how much to share, and principals could then decide whether to retain the agent or not. When an agent shared nothing, then that agent was chosen in the next round ninety-three percent of the time. For the agent sharing five dollars, retention dropped to thirty-nine percent in this experiment.[39] In the survey component of this research, and disconcertingly, principals who got others to be selfish on their behalf tended to give their own

---

[37] Sharon's Knesset Address, September 22, 1982. https://mfa.gov.il/MFA/ForeignPolicy/MFADocuments/Yearbook6/Pages/83%20Statement%20in%20the%20Knesset%20by%20Defense%20Minister%20Sh.aspx.

[38] John R. Hamman, George Loewenstein, and Roberto A. Weber, "Self-Interest through Delegation: An Additional Rationale for the Principal-Agent Relationship," *American Economic Review* 100, no. 4 (2010): 1843.

[39] Ibid., p. 1833.

conduct a pass. They perceived their own behavior more favorably. In turn, the agents absolved themselves of guilt as well. The agents could attribute their hard-heartedness to the incentive structure in which they were placed. And in choosing who to hold responsible, the principal or the agent, recipients tended to blame the latter.

Other experiments show that delegating unfair decisions shifts the victim's attribution of responsibility from the principal to the agent.[40] The latter is most likely to be punished for the unfair decision, should it come to that. These experiments and surveys suggest that delegation may relieve a principal of both the external and internal consequences of immoral actions. Externally, blame, shame, and punishment falls on the agent. Internally, the burden of guilt lifts. Delegation warps the attribution of blame and punishment. It may help to protect your position and reputation. These experiments suggest that delegation protects, in addition, your psychological disposition. It is an underexamined, devious route, if not to happiness, to a place that limits the misery of shame. But agents vary. Eric Fair, not a participant in the economists' experiments, could find no moral detachment and psychological relief in the role of the agent.

8

With *won't control,* the potential psychological distance stretches beyond what obtains in the lab experiment. In the lab, everyone seeks financial gain. Unavailable to the experimental principal is the distinct, abhorrent, perhaps even unknowable motivation that the agent brings with him, and that the *won't control* principal can condemn and describe as an unstoppable force, independent of and quite separate from his motivations. Montcalm set "in motion an engine, which it exceeds human power to control." In pointing to this "engine" as a force of nature beyond human power, the *won't control* principal puts himself at a further remove from the selfish and

---

[40] Björn Bartling and Urs Fischbacher, "Shifting the Blame: On Delegation and Responsibility," *The Review of Economic Studies* 79, no. 1 (2012): 67–87.

immoral actions of the agent. In much of the principal–agent literature, principals seek agents who are allied in their preferences. Here
the principal is not seeking a close "ally" and selecting an agent with
similar preferences. He is selecting an agent with usefully different
preferences. At Fort William Henry we have agents with a particular
taste for cruelty, juxtaposed with the preferences of a Christian principal. In Beirut, the Christian militia's motivations were unknown
to the principal: beyond Sharon's "worst dreams." Under these
conditions, the principal is yet more tempted to rationalize his role,
to assert *can't control*, and to wriggle off the moral hook.

Accountability requires an accurate report of what happened and
some punishment for the wrongdoing that occurred. In shifting
accountability for exhaust fumes or atrocities onto rogue agents,
principals may expect to escape some political or legal punishment imposed by others. They are also less likely to punish themselves. With blame, leaders have one task they always seem willing
to delegate. We may not expect more from business executives and
politicians, but even courageous and battle-hardened leaders leave
"the horror of blameworthiness" to their agents.

7
Conclusion

Even marooned like Robinson Crusoe, we seek to delegate. We might expect intimate and precious tasks to be closely held, yet there are markets for all sorts of services. While governments are less likely to outsource sovereign tasks, where the risk of betrayal has survival-threatening consequences, there is, nevertheless, a demand for biker gangs, vigilantes, war lords, and local warriors. It is difficult to locate clear boundaries to delegation, and as the study of delegation and happiness pointed out, some with the option to do so do not delegate as much as they should. But if there is an iron law to delegation, then blame is one task that will be delegated.

The actors in delegation relationships are motivated by a range of incentives, come in small or large numbers, and as individuals or organizations in private and public life. For all the variation, there is a clear underlying structure to these relationships. Principal-agent theory points to the conflicting preferences of the actors, the availability of information, the presence of opportunism, and the issue of control. While much of the theoretical work is formal, given the pervasiveness of these relationships and the insights offered into a variety of seemingly unrelated real-world problems, there is value in developing the logic of delegation outside its familiar territory and beyond the usual bounds of economic analysis.

Going back and forth between the theory and a variety of examples generates puzzles about why, for example, in some organizational contexts principals refuse to punish rogue agents, or whether the principal is refusing rather than losing control. In thinking about these puzzles, I have tried to be as sparing as possible with additional complications and concepts. This modified logic of delegation differs from the standard account in the treatment of the main parties to

Why Delegate?. Neil J. Mitchell, Oxford University Press (2021). © Oxford University Press.
DOI: 10.1093/oso/9780190904197.003.0007

the relationship. The principal turns out to be a more untrustworthy figure in her relationship with the agents. The agent, most likely a professional agent, is capable of more than narrow self-interest, may develop feelings for fellow agents, and may shape his preferences by the esteem of his colleagues and the pull of loyalty. Furthermore, he may be taken advantage of when it comes to allocating the blame. In contrast to his conventional depiction as the fount of opportunism in the relationship, in some contexts he may turn out to be a more sympathetic figure.

The accepted version of principal-agent theory provides an important, but partial account of the delegation relationships encountered in practice. It assumes conflicting goals and informational differences. As Laffont and Martimort write, "conflicting objectives and decentralized information are thus the two basic ingredients of incentive theory. The essential paradigm for the analysis of market behavior by economists is one where economic agents pursue, at least to some extent, their private interests."[1] The principal wants work and the agent wants to shirk. The agent knows more than the principal, both about what he will bring to the relationship in the first place and what effort he exerts once in the relationship. Conflicting preferences, in combination with this informational imbalance, produce the likelihood of opportunism by the agent and control problems for the principal. The principal takes measures to deal with the untrustworthy agent. If the agent survives the selection process, agrees to undertake the task, and then monitoring reveals a lack of effort or misdirected effort, he may be punished or the relationship terminated.

A broader and more serviceable logic of delegation includes incentives to delegate beyond efficiency gains, examines systematic and tenacious agent resistance to control, and recognizes the complexities of administering punishment. Opportunism is on both sides of the relationship. Agents have problems with principals and are shocked by their opportunistic behavior, as a VW software

---

[1] Laffont and Martimort (2002), p. 2.

engineer who thought the defeat device had been approved must have been shocked in the autumn of 2015 when VW bosses testified before Congress about their lack of information about the defeat device, or as Eric Fair was when he saw the *60 Minutes* portrayal of what had happened at Abu Ghraib in the spring of 2004 as a simple principal-agent problem. In other contexts, principals may set out to select agents with the blame in mind. In addition to principals who *can't control*, there are those that *won't control*. Preferences can differ, but not necessarily conflict. The agent's private gain or understanding of his mission may be different from and at the same time instrumental to the principal's strategic goal. Beyond conflicting interests, principal-agent theory assumes the principal suffers from information disadvantages. Sometimes the principal pretends to suffer in this way. Both sides can lack relevant information about the relationship, and both sides can be untrustworthy. While *won't control* is by design difficult to disentangle from *can't control*, it does not defy empirical investigation. There are some clear tell-tale indicators that may be usefully derived from principal-agent theory, and there has to be some plausible strategic goal served by agents "shirking" and acting in a self-interested, immoral, or controversial way.

The substantive preferences of agents may be complex. The theory, even in a modified form, is not very informative in itself. The examples in this book suggest that in practice the private goods sought by agents are diverse and sometimes obscure, be it the satisfaction of a "God complex," Sepp Blatter's Nobel Peace Prize, violence for its own sake, or where self-esteem is vested in peer-esteem. Whether or not the exact form of gratification is pinned down, the important point is that the agent may have preferences different from the principal and powerful enough to produce action on his own behalf.

From the beginning, scholars have been concerned with the realities of the delegation relationship and how it works out in practice. Principal-agent theorists have shown that the uncertainties about who is charge, which is central to the delegation relationship, may be mitigated by professionalism. The identity and idealism of the agent, which is shaped by the training undergone by the agent,

influence the agent's efforts. Scholars have emphasized the importance of non-monetary incentives for the agent, and of extending
the description of the principal-agent relationship in this way. In his
observations on the medical profession, Kenneth Arrow argued that
theoretical work had to find a place for social obligations and professional responsibility as a mechanism to overcome the trust gap
in a delegation relationship. Others have emphasized this moral,
idealistic, or honor element in agent behavior both in theory and in
policy applications. But professionalism is not an unmitigated good.

Overlooked are the side effects of professionalism, where the
loyalties it fosters among members of a profession motivate them
to herd together with rogue agents. These professionals may be in
positions of great trust and responsibility. As a consequence, opportunistic behavior carries a risk of severe harm. Even with unspeakable abuse and murder, these agents put their loyalties to each other
over the service they are supposed to provide. This strong feeling of
group-belonging among difficult-to-replace agents produces passivity in the principal. The principal in charge of multiple agents is
constrained by the fear that punishing misconduct may create disillusionment, lower levels of effort, walls of silence, and even mutiny in the ranks. Leaders' responses to abuse in the Catholic Church
and war crimes in the military are examples of the malign effect
of this agent confidence factor. Hierarchical structures with single
principals and multiple agents, who are in possession of specialized
training, difficult-to-replace skills, and a feeling of community in
some higher group purpose fit the profile of organizations susceptible to passivity in the chain of delegation. It is in pronounced form
in the institutions that were looked at here, but other security and
police forces and other religions beyond the Catholic may find punishment a complicated process. Even the medical profession, which
is more likely to be dealing with agents misleading principals about
their level of competence, rather than opportunism motivated by
deviant preferences (as described in Chapter 3), may find it difficult
to discipline their own, not just out of concern for the reputation
of the hospital, but for the signal that punishment sends to other
practitioners.

The solution to this sort of problem lies, in part, in selection and in more professionalism. These agents normally follow a code that checks opportunism and reduces the need for monitoring and financial incentives. The code must feature ranking loyalty to the values of the profession over loyalty to misbehaving fellow professionals, which extends to those in charge. As Eric Fair told me, loyalty bonds in an army should be hard to break, but at the same time they must not get in the way of maintaining the integrity of the institution, which tests the leadership of those in charge. For those in charge, the cost of deciding not to take charge needs to increase. Externally, outside the delegation relationship, having governments live up to their democratic duties to provide the constitutional and practical protection required for an active civil society that creates third-party monitoring is essential in holding professionals and other difficult-to-control agents accountable across the issues discussed here, from child abuse to willful environmental degradation by car companies. Effective monitoring is challenging, even with an active civil society. It took a long time to discover VW's cheating chip.

The world turns on the delegation relationship, which may lead to happiness or misery. All sorts of problems can benefit from attention to who is doing what for whom. All the same, you will have concluded some pages back that the logic of delegation is not a theory of everything. Perhaps it is a mundane take on Constantin Levin's problems in *Anna Karenina*. But it helps to simplify the forces at work in a swath of important human interactions. In that sense, it is a theory of quite a lot.

Bibliography

Agrawal, Anup, and Tareque Nasser, "Blockholders on Boards and CEO Compensation, Turnover and Firm Valuation," *Quarterly Journal of Finance 9*, no. 3 (2019): 1–67.

Agrawal, Anup, and Tommy Cooper, "Corporate Governance Consequences of Accounting Scandals: Evidence from Top Management CEO and Auditor Turnover," *Quarterly Journal of Finance 7*, no. 1 (2016): 1–41.

Aikins, Mattieu. "The A-Team Killings," *Rolling Stone*, November 6, 2013.

Aitken Report: An Investigation into Cases of Deliberate Abuse and Unlawful Killing in Iraq in 2003 and 2004 (The British Army, January 25, 2008). http://image.guardian.co.uk/sys-files/Guardian/documents/2008/01/25/aitken_rep.pdf (accessed September 21, 2018).

Akerlof, George A., "The Market for "Lemons": Quality Uncertainty and the Market Mechanism," *The Quarterly Journal of Economics 84*, no. 3 (1970): 488–500.

Akerlof, George A., and Rachel E. Kranton, *Identity Economics: How Our Identities Shape Our Work, Wages, and Well-Being* (Princeton, NJ: Princeton University Press, 2010).

Alter, Karen, "Delegation to International Courts and the Limits of Re-contracting Political Power," in *Delegation and Agency in International Organizations*, edited by Darren A. Hawkins, David A. Lake, Daniel L. Nielson, and Michael J. Tierney (Cambridge: Cambridge University Press, 2006), pp. 312–338.

Amnesty International, *Left in The Dark: Failures of Accountability for Civilian Casualties Caused by International Military Operations in Afghanistan* (London: Amnesty International, 2014) https://www.amnesty.org.nz/left-dark-failures-accountability-civilian-casualties-caused-international-military-operations (accessed August 14, 2018).

Amnesty International, *Stars on their Shoulders. Blood on their Hands: War Crimes Committed by the Nigerian Military* (London: Amnesty International, 2015). https://www.amnesty.org/download/Documents/AFR4416572015ENGLISH.PDF (accessed June 13, 2018).

Amnesty International, *Amnesty International Report 2015–2016: The State of the World's Human Rights* (London: Amnesty International, 2016).

Anderson, David, *Histories of the Hanged: The Dirty War in Kenya and the End of Empire* (London: W. W. Norton. 2005).

Anglo-Irish Treaty, December 6, 1921. http://treaty.nationalarchives.ie/document-gallery/anglo-irish-treaty-6-december-1921/ (accessed September 21, 2018).

Appeal. *In the Matter of Ray Rice* (November 28, 2014). https://s3.amazonaws.com/s3.documentcloud.org/documents/1372767/judge-ruling-ray-rice-decision.pdf (accessed September 7, 2017).

Arrow, Kenneth J., "The Economics of Agency," in *Principals and Agents: The Structure of Business*, edited by John W. Pratt and Richard Zeckhauser (Boston: Harvard Business School Press, 1985), pp. 37–51.

Arrow, Kenneth, "Uncertainty and the Welfare Economics of Medical Care," *The American Economic Review* 53, no. 5 (December 1963): 941–973.

Baha Mousa Inquiry, General Sir Mike Jackson, Hearing Transcript. http://webarchive.nationalarchives.gov.uk/20120215203912/http://www.bahamousainquiry.org/ (accessed July 6, 2018).

Bakke, Kristin M., Neil J. Mitchell, and Hannah M. Smidt, "When States Crack Down on Human Rights Defenders," *International Studies Quarterly* 64, no. 1 (March 2020): 85–96.

Banks, Jeffrey, and Barry Weingast, "The Political Control of Bureaucracies under Asymmetric Information," *American Journal of Political Science* 36, no. 2 (May 1992): 509–524.

Bartling, Björn, and Urs Fischbacher, "Shifting the Blame: On Delegation and Responsibility," *The Review of Economic Studies* 79, no. 1 (January 2012): 67–87.

Bates, Robert, *When Things Fell Apart: State Failure in Late Twentieth Century Africa* (Cambridge: Cambridge University Press 2008).

Bénabou, Roland, and Jean Tirole, "Intrinsic and Extrinsic Motivation," *Review of Economic Studies* 70, no. 3 (July 2003): 489–520.

Bendor, Jon, Amihai Glazer, and Thomas H. Hammond, "Theories of Delegation," *Annual Review of Political Science* 4 (2001): 235–269.

Bennett, Huw, *Fighting the Mau Mau* (Cambridge: Cambridge University Press, 2012).

Bennett, Richard, *The Black and Tans* (Barnsley, UK: Pen and Sword Books, 2010 [1959]).

Bernhagen, Patrick, and Neil J. Mitchell, "The Private Provision of Public Goods," *International Studies Quarterly* 54, no. 4 (December 2010): 1175–1187.

Blake, Heidi, and Jonathan Calvert, *The Ugly Game: The Qatari Plot to Buy the World Cup* (London: Simon & Schuster, 2015).

Blakeley, Ruth, and Sam Raphael, "Accountability, Denial and the Future-Proofing of British Torture," *International Affairs* 96, no. 3 (May 2020): 691–709.

Bohara, Alok K., Neil J. Mitchell, Mani Nepal, and Nejem Raheem, "Human Rights Violations, Corruption, and the Policy of Repression," *The Policy Studies Journal* 36, no. 1 (2008): 1–18.

Borzyskowski, Inken von, and Felicity Vabulas, "Credible Commitments? Explaining IGO Suspensions to Sanction Political Backsliding," *International Studies Quarterly* 63, no. 1 (March 2019): 139–152.

Boudreaux, Christopher J., Gokhan Karahan, and R. Morris Coats, "Bend It like FIFA: Corruption on and off the Pitch," *Managerial Finance* 42, no. 9 (2016): 866–878.

Branch, Daniel, *Defeating Mau Mau, Creating Kenya* (Cambridge: Cambridge University Press, 2009).

Brehm, John, and Scott Gates, *Working, Shirking, and Sabotage: Bureaucratic Response to a Democratic Public* (Ann Arbor: University of Michigan Press, 1997).

Brysk, Alyson, *Speaking Rights to Power: Constructing Political Will* (Oxford: Oxford University Press, 2013).

Bueno de Mesquita, Bruce, George W. Downs, Alastair Smith, and Feryal Marie Cherif, "Thinking Inside the Box: A Closer Look at Democracy and Human Rights," *International Studies Quarterly* 49, no. 3 (2005): 439–457.

Butler, Christopher K., Tali Gluch and Neil J. Mitchell, "Security Forces and Sexual Violence: A Cross-National Analysis of a Principal–– Agent Argument," *Journal of Peace Research*, 44, no. 6, (2007): 669–687.

Callwell, C. E., *Field-Marshal Sir Henry Wilson: His Life and Diaries*, vol. II (London: Cassell and Company, 1927).

Carey, Sabine C., Michael P. Colaresi, and Neil J. Mitchell, "Governments, Informal Links to Militias, and Accountability," *Journal of Conflict Resolution* 59, no. 5 (August 2015): 850–876.

Carey, Sabine C., Michael P. Colaresi, and Neil J. Mitchell, "Risk Mitigation, Regime Security, and Militias: Beyond Coup-Proofing," *International Studies Quarterly* 60, no. 1 (March 2016): 59–72.

Carey, Sabine C., and Neil J. Mitchell, "Progovernment Militias," *Annual Review of Political Science* 20 (2017): 127–147.

Carey, Sabine C., Neil J. Mitchell, and Will Lowe, "States, the Security Sector, and the Monopoly of Violence: A New Database on Pro-Government Militias," *Journal of Peace Research* 50, no. 2 (March 2013): 249–258.

Carlson, Kyle, Joshua Kim, Annamaria Lusard, and Colin F. Camerer, "Bankruptcy Rates among NFL Players with Short-Lived Income Spikes," *American Economic Review* 105, no. 5 (2015): 381–384.

Cingranelli, David L., and Mikhail Filippov, "Electoral Rules and Incentives to Protect Human Rights," *Journal of Politics* 72, no. 1 (January 2010): 243–257.

CNN. "Sick, Dying and Raped in America's Nursing Hopes" (2017). http://edition. cnn.com/interactive/2017/02/health/nursing-home-sex-abuse-investigation/ (accessed June 15, 2018).

Cobain, Ian, *The History Thieves: Secret, Lies and the Shaping of a Modern Nation* (London: Portobello Books, 2016).

Cobain, Ian, *Anatomy of a Killing: Life and Death on A Divided Island* (London: Granta, 2020).

Cohen, Dara Kay, *Rape during Civil War* (Ithaca, NY: Cornell University Press, 2016).

Cohen, Dara Kay, and Ragnhild Nordås, "Do States Delegate Shameful Violence to Militias? Patterns of Sexual Violence in Recent Armed Conflicts," *Journal of Conflict Resolution* 59, no. 1 (August 2015): 877–898.

Cole, Wade M., "Sovereignty Relinquished? Explaining Commitment to the International Human Rights Covenants, 1966–1999," *American Sociological Review* 70, no. 3 (June 2005): 472–495.

Conn, David, *The Fall of the House of FIFA* (London: Yellow Jersey Press, 2016).

Costa, Dora, and Matthew Kahn, *Heroes and Cowards: The Social Face of War* (Princeton, NJ: Princeton University Press, 2008).

Cox, Eric, "State Interests and the Creation and Functioning of the United Nations Human Rights Council," *Journal of International Law and International Relations* 6, no. 1 (Summer 2010): 87–120.

Defoe, Daniel, *The Life and Adventures of Robinson Crusoe* (London: MacMillan and Co., [1719] 1866), p. 212.

Dingemans, James. "Review of the Allegations of Misconduct in Relation to the FA's 2018 World Cup Bid" (2011). http://www.FIFA.com/mm/document/affederation/administration/01/44/40/85/jdqcreview-summary.pdf (accessed November 7, 2017).

Dixit, Avinash, "Incentives and Organizations in the Public Sector: An Interpretative Review," *The Journal of Human Resources* 37, no. 4 (2002): 696–727.

Duflo, Esther, Michael Greenstone, Rohini Pande and Nicholas Ryan, "Truth-Telling by Third-Party Auditors and the Response of Polluting Firms: Experimental Evidence from India," Massachusetts Institute of Technology, Department of Economics Working Paper Series (July 17, 2013).

Eisenhardt, Kathleen M., "Building Theories from Case Study Research," *The Academy of Management Review* 14, no. 4 (October 1989): 532–550.

Elsig, Manfred, and Mark Pollack, "Agents, Trustees and International Courts: The Politics of Judicial Appointments at the World Trade Organization," *European Journal of International Relations* 20, no. 2 (2014): 391–495.

Elster, Jon, *Ulysses and the Sirens* (Cambridge: Cambridge University Press, 1984).

Fair, Eric, *Consequence: A Memoir* (New York: Henry Holt, 2016).

Fama, Eugene, "Agency Problems and the Theory of the Firm," *The Journal of Political Economy* 88, no. 2 (April 1980): 288–307.

Fama, Eugene, and Michael C. Jensen, "The Separation of Ownership and Control," *The Journal of Law and Economics* 26, no. 2 (June 1983): 301–325.

Fariss, Christopher J., "Respect for Human Rights Has Improved over Time: Modeling the Changing Standard of Accountability," *American Political Science Review* 108, no. 2 (May 2014): 297–318.

Feaver, Peter, *Armed Servants: Agency, Oversight, and Civil Military Relations* (Cambridge, MA: Harvard University Press, 2003).

Fedorowich, Kent, "The Problems of Disbandment: The Royal Ulster Constabulary and Imperial Migration, 1919–29." *Irish Historical Studies* 30, no. 117 (May 1996): 88–110.

Fenimore Cooper, James, *The Last of the Mohicans* (New York: Penguin Books, 1986).

FIFA. "Victim Statement and Request for Restitution" (2016). http://resources.FIFA.com/mm/Document/AFFederation/FootballGovernance/02/77/05/38/FIFARestitutionRequest_Neutral.pdf (accessed November 7, 2017).

Fiorina, Morris P., "Legislative Choice of Regulatory Forms: Legal Process or Administrative Process?" *Public Choice* 39, no. 1 (1982): 33–66.

Freud, Sigmund, *Group Psychology and the Analysis of the Ego* (London: W.W. Norton, [1921] 1975).

Garber, Alan M., and Jonathan Skinner, "Is American Health Care Uniquely Inefficient?" *Journal of Economic Perspectives: A Journal of the American Economic Association* 22, no. 4 (Fall 2008): 27–50.

Garcia, Michael. "Report on the Inquiry into the 2018/2022 FIFA World Cup Bidding Process" (2014). http://www.fifa.com/governance/news/y=2017/m=6/news=fifa-statement-on-recent-media-coverage-regarding-the-garcia-report-2898791.html (accessed November 24, 2017).

Garriga, Ana C., "Human Rights Regimes, Reputation, and Foreign Direct Investment," *International Studies Quarterly* 60, no. 1 (March 2016): 160–172.

Gibbon, Edward, *The History of the Decline and Fall of the Roman Empire*, vol. I (London: The Folio Society, 1983).

Gibney, Mark, Linda Cornett, Reed Wood, Peter Haschke, and Daniel Arnon, *The Political Terror Scale 1976–2015* (2015). http://www.politicalterrorscale.org.

Gilardi, Fabrizio, *Delegation in the Regulatory State: Independent Regulatory Agencies in Western Europe* (Cheltenham, UK: Edward Elgar, 2008).

The Government Accountability Office, "Elder Abuse." United States Government GAO-17-33 (2016).

Hamman, John R., George Loewenstein, and Roberto A. Weber, "Self-Interest through Delegation: An Additional Rationale for the Principal-Agent Relationship," *American Economic Review* 100, no. 4 (September 2010): 1826–1846.

Hart, Oliver, *Firms, Contracts and Financial Structure* (Oxford: Clarendon Press, 1995).

Hart, Oliver, "Incomplete Contracts and Control," *American Economic Review* 107, no. 7 (July 2017): 1731–1752.

Hartzband, Pamela, and Jerome Groopman, "Money and the Changing Culture of Medicine," *The New England Journal of Medicine* 360 (January 2009): 101–103.

Hartzband, Pamela, and Jerome Groopman, "How to Fix Our Health Care System," *New York Review of Books* 64 (July 2017): 47–50.

Hastings, Max, *Vietnam: An Epic Tragedy, 1945-1974* (London: William Collins, 2018).

Hastings, Max, "Wrath of the Centurions," *London Review of Books*, January 25, 2018: 19–22.

Hawkins, Darren, David Lake, Daniel Nielson, and Michael J. Tierney, *Delegation and Agency in International Organizations* (Cambridge: Cambridge University Press, 2006).

Hill, Christopher, *Milton and the English Revolution* (London: Faber and Faber, 1977).

Holmstrom, Bengt, "Pay for Performance and Beyond," *American Economic Review* 107, no. 7 (July 2017): 1753–1777.

House of Commons, *Parliamentary Debates*, vol. 135 (1920).

House of Commons. "Written Evidence Submitted by the *Sunday Times*," *Culture, Media and Sport Committee* (May 9, 2011). https://publications.parliament.uk/pa/cm201012/cmselect/cmcumeds/1031/1031we02.htm.

House of Commons. "Professor Miguel Maduro Oral Evidence: Sports Governance," Digital, Culture, Media and Sport Committee, House of Commons 320 (September 13, 2017). https://old.parliament.uk/business/committees/committees-a-z/commons-select/culture-media-and-sport-committee/news-parliament-2017/170912-sports-governance-evidence/.

Human Rights Watch, *World Report* (2015) https://www.hrw.org/world-report/2015 (accessed April 18, 2016).

Human Rights Watch, "Follow the Thread: The Need for Supply Chain Transparency in the Garment and Footwear Industry" (April 20, 2017). https://www.hrw.org/report/2017/04/20/follow-thread/need-supply-chain-transparency-garment-and-footwear-industry (accessed December 22, 2017).

Hume, David, "Of the First Principles of Government," in *Hume's Moral and Political Philosophy*, edited by Henry D. Aiken (New York: Hafner Press, 1948), pp. 307–310.

International Crisis Group, "The Future of the Afghan Local Police," Asia Report No. 268 (June 4, 2015): 1–27.

International Crisis Group, "Watchmen of Lake Chad: Vigilante Groups Fighting Boko Haram," *Africa Report* 244 (February 23, 2017): 1–30.

Jensen, Michael C., "The Modern Industrial Revolution, Exit, and the Failure of Internal Control Systems," *The Journal of Finance* 48, no. 3 (1993): 831–880.

Jensen, Michael C., and William H. Meckling, "Theory of the Firm: Managerial Behavior, Agency Costs and Ownership Structure," *Journal of Financial Economics* 3, no. 4 (October 1976): 305–360.

Jones, Howard, *My Lai:Vietnam, 1968, and the Descent into Darkness* (New York: Oxford University Press, 2017).

Kahan Commission, "The Beirut Massacre: The Complete Kahan Commission Report" (New York: Karz-Cohl, 1983).

Kelman, Herbert C., and V. Lee Hamilton, *Crimes of Obedience: Toward a Social Psychology of Authority and Responsibility* (New Haven, CT: Yale University Press, 1989).

Kennedy, Sir Ian, "Review of the Response of Heart of England NHS Foundation Trust to Concerns about Mr. Ian Paterson's Surgical Practice" (2013). https://hgs.uhb.nhs.uk/wp-content/uploads/Kennedy-Report-Final.pdf (accessed July 10, 2017).

Kiewiet, D. Roderick, and Mathew D. McCubbins, *The Logic of Delegation: Congressional Parties and the Appropriations Process* (Chicago: University of Chicago Press, 1991).

Krain, Matthew M., "*J'accuse*! Does Naming and Shaming Perpetrators Reduce the Severity of Genocides or Politicides?," *International Studies Quarterly* 56, no. 3 (September 2012): 574–589.

Lachs, Mark S., and Karl A. Pillemer, "Elder Abuse," *New England Journal of Medicine* 373 (November 2015): 1947–1956.

Laffont, Jean-Jacques, and David Martimort, *The Theory of Economic Incentives: The Principal Agent Model* (Princeton, NJ: Princeton University Press, 2002).

Laird, Melvin, *With Honor* (Madison: University of Wisconsin Press, 2008).

Lake, David A., and Mathew D. McCubbins, "The Logic of Delegation to International Organizations," in *Delegation and Agency in International Organizations,* edited by Darren A. Hawkins, David A. Lake, Daniel L. Nielson, and Michael J. Tierney (Cambridge, UK: Cambridge University Press, 2006): 341–368.

Landman, Todd, *Protecting Human Rights: A Comparative Study* (Washington, DC: Georgetown University Press, 2005).

Landman, Todd, *Human Rights and Democracy: The Precarious Triumph of Ideals* (London: Bloomsbury, 2013).

Langewiesche, William, "How One U.S. Soldier Blew the Whistle on a Cold-Blooded War Crime," *Vanity Fair,* June 16, 2015. https://www.vanityfair.com/news/2015/06/iraq-war-crime-army-cunningham-hatley-trial (accessed November 9, 2020).

Lauren, Paul Gordon, "To Preserve and Build on Its Achievements and to Redress Its Shortcomings: The Journey from the Commission on Human Rights to the Human Rights Council," *Human Rights Quarterly* 29, no. 2 (May 2007): 307–345.

Lebovic, James H., and Erik Voeten, "The Politics of Shame: The Condemnation of Country Human Rights Practices in the UNCHR," *International Studies Quarterly* 50, no. 4 (December 2006): 861–888.

Ledwidge, Frank, *Losing Small Wars: British Military Failure in Iraq and Afghanistan* (New Haven, CT: Yale University Press 2012).

Li, Yongbin, Jing Xu Fang Wang, Bin Wang, et al., "Overprescribing in China, Driven by Financial Incentives, Results in Very High Use of Antibiotics, Injections, and Corticosteroids," *Health Affairs* 31, no. 5 (2012): 1075–1082.

Locke, Richard M., Fei Qin, and Alberto Brause, "Does Monitoring Improve Labor Standards? Lessons from Nike," *Industrial and Labor Relations Review* 61, no. 1 (October 2007): 1–31.

Lund-Thomsen, Peter and Adam Lindgreen, "Corporate Social Responsibility in Global Value Chains: Where Are We Now and Where Are We Going?," *Journal of Business Ethics* 123, no. 1 (2014): 11–22.

Mayer, Kenneth, "Closing Military Bases (Finally): Solving Collective Dilemmas Through Delegation," *Legislative Studies Quarterly* 20, no. 3 (August 1995): 393–413.

McCubbins, Mathew D., and Thomas Schwartz, "Congressional Oversight Overlooked: Police Patrols versus Fire Alarms," *American Journal of Political Science* 28, no. 1 (February 1984): 165–179.

McCubbins, Matthew, Roger G. Noll, and Barry R. Weingast, "Administrative Procedures as Instruments of Political Control," *Journal of Law Economics and Organization* 3, no. 2 (Fall 1987): 243–277.

McKee, Ann C., et al., "Clinicopathological Evaluation of Chronic Traumatic Encephalopathy in Players of American Football," *Journal of the American Medical Association* 318, no. 4 (July 2017): 360–370.

McPherson, Kim, Giorgia Gon, and Maggie Scott, "International Variations in a Selected Number of Surgical Procedures," *OECD Health Working Papers* 61 (Paris: OECD, 2013).

Meernik, James, Rosa Aloisi, Marsha Sowell, and Angela Nichols, "The Impact of Human Rights Organizations on Naming and Shaming," *Journal of Conflict Resolution* 56, no. 2 (April 2012): 233–256.

Mill, John Stuart, *Considerations on Representative Government* (Rockville, MD: Serenity, [1861] 2008).

Miller, Gary J., "The Political Evolution of Principal-Agent Models," *Annual Review of Political Science* 8 (2005): 203–225.

Miller, Gary J., and Andrew B. Whitford, *Above Politics: Bureaucratic Discretion and Credible Commitment* (Cambridge: Cambridge University Press, 2015).

Milton, John, "The Doctrine and Discipline of Divorce," in *John Milton Prose: Major Writings on Liberty, Politics, Religion, and Education*, edited by David Loewenstein (Oxford: Wiley-Blackwell, [1643] 2013).

Milton, John, "The Tenure of Kings and Magistrates," in *John Milton Prose: Major Writings on Liberty, Politics, Religion, and Education*, edited by David Loewenstein (Oxford: Wiley-Blackwell, [1650] 2013).

Milton, John, "A Second Defence of the English People," in *John Milton Prose: Major Writings on Liberty, Politics, Religion, and Education*, edited by David Loewenstein (Oxford: Wiley-Blackwell, [1654] 2013).

Mitchell, Neil J., *Agents of Atrocity: Leaders, Followers, and the Violation of Human Rights in Civil War* (New York: Palgrave Macmillan, 2004).

Mitchell, Neil J., *Democracy's Blameless Leaders: From Dresden to Abu Ghraib, How Leaders Evade Accountability for Abuse Atrocity and Killing* (New York: New York University Press, 2012).

Mitchell, Neil J., Sabine C. Carey, and Christopher K. Butler, "The Impact of Pro-government Militias on Human Rights Violations," *International Interactions* 40, no. 5 (November 2014): 812–836.

Mosley, Layna, and David A. Singer, "Migration, Labor, and the International Political Economy," *Annual Review of Political Science* 18 (2015): 283–301.

National Commission on Physician Payment Reform Report (2013). http://physicianpaymentcommission.org.

Nelson, Deborah, *The War behind Me: Vietnam Veterans Confront the Truth about U.S. War Crimes* (New York: Basic Books, 2008).

Nielsen, Richard A., and Beth A. Simmons, "Rewards for Ratification: Payoffs for Participating in the International Human Rights Regime?" *International Studies Quarterly* 59, no. 2 (June 2015): 197–208.

North, Douglas, John Wallis, and Barry Weingast, *Violence and Social Orders: A Conceptual Framework for Interpreting Recorded Human History* (Cambridge: Cambridge University Press, 2009).

Olson, Mancur, *The Logic of Collective Action: Public Good and the Theory of Groups* (Cambridge, MA: Harvard University Press, 1965).

Perkins, Kieran M., Sheree L. Boulet, Denise J. Jamieson, and Dmitriy M. Kissin, "Trends and Outcomes of Gestational Surrogacy in the United States," *Fertility and Sterility* 106, no. 2 (August 2016): 435–442.

Persson, Anna, Bo Rothstein, and Jan Teorell, "Why Anticorruption Reforms Fail—Systemic Corruption as a Collective Action Problem," *Governance: An*

International Journal of Policy, Administration, and Institutions 26, no. 3 (July 2013): 449–471.

Poynter, Gavin, "Emotions in the Labour Process," *European Journal of Psychotherapy, Counselling & Health* 5, no. 3 (2002): 247–261.

Rasul, Imran, and Daniel Rogger, "Management of Bureaucrats and Public Service Delivery: Evidence from the Nigerian Civil Service," *The Economic Journal* 128 no. 608 (February 2018): 413–446.

Rehfeld, Andrew, "Representation Rethought: On Trustees, Delegates, and Gyroscopes in the Study of Political Representation and Democracy," *American Political Science Review* 103, no. 2 (May 2009): 214–230.

Rhee, Robert J., "The Madoff Scandal: Market Regulatory Failure and the Business Education of Lawyers," *The Journal of Corporation Law* 35, no. 2 (2009): 363–392.

Risse, Thomas, Stephen C. Ropp, and Kathryn Sikkink, *The Power of Human Rights: International Norms and Domestic Change* (Cambridge: Cambridge University Press, 1999).

Royal Commission into Institutional Responses to Child Abuse, Final Report. https://www.childabuseroyalcommission.gov.au (accessed November 9, 2020).

Ruggie, John Gerard, "Reconstituting the Global Public Domain: Issues, Actors, and Practices," *European Journal of International Relations* 10, no. 4 (December 2004): 499–531.

Schneider, Gerald, Lilli Banholzer, and Laura Albarracin, "Ordered Rape: A Principal-Agent Analysis of Wartime Sexual Violence in the DR Congo," *Violence Against Women* 21 (2015): 1341–1363.

Schroeder, Steven A., and William Frist, "Phasing Out Fee-For-Service Payment," *New England Journal of Medicine* 368 (May 2013): 2029–2032.

Securities and Exchange Commission, Office of Investigations. Investigation of Failure of the SEC to Uncover Bernard Madoff's Ponzi Scheme. Report No. OIG-509 (2009). https://www.sec.gov/news/studies/2009/oig-509.pdf (accessed July 21, 2017).

Segev, Tom, *One Palestine Complete: Jews and Arabs Under the British Mandate*, trans. Hiam Watzman (New York: Metropolitan Books, 2000).

Sharon's Knesset Address, September 22, 1982. https://mfa.gov.il/MFA/ForeignPolicy/MFADocuments/Yearbook6/Pages/83%20Statement%20in%20the%20Knesset%20by%20Defense%20Minister%20Sh.aspx (accessed November 9, 2020).

Shleifer, Andrei and Robert W. Vishny, "A Survey of Corporate Governance," *The Journal of Finance* 52, no. 2 (1997): 737–783.

Simmons, Beth, *Mobilizing for Human Rights* (Cambridge: Cambridge University Press, 2009).

Sipe, A. W. Richard, Thomas Doyle, and Patrick J. Wall, *Sex, Priests, and Secret Codes: The Catholic Church's 2,000 Year Paper Trail of Sexual Abuse* (London: Crux, [2005] 2016).

Slate, "Is a Surrogate a Mother?" February 15, 2016. http://www.slate.com/articles/double_x/doublex/2016/02/custody_case_over_triplets_in_california_ raises_questions_about_surrogacy.html?via=gdpr-consent (accessed December 22, 2017).

Smerdon, Usha Rengachary, "Crossing Bodies, Crossing Borders: International Surrogacy between the United States and India," *Cumberland Law Review* 39, no. 1 (2008): 15–85.

Smidt, Hannah M., Dominic Perera, Neil J. Mitchell, and Kristin M. Bakke, "Silencing Their Critics: How Government Restrictions against Civil Society Affect International 'Naming and Shaming,'" *British Journal of Political Science* online (February 2020): 1–22.

Smith, Adam. *The Theory of Moral Sentiments* (New York: Prometheus Books, [1759] 2000).

Steele, Ian K., *Betrayals: Fort William Henry and the "Massacre"* (New York: Oxford University Press, 1990).

Strom, Kaare, "Delegation and Accountability in Parliamentary Democracies," *European Journal of Political Research* 37, no. 3 (May 2000): 261–289.

Strom, Kaare, Wolfgang C. Müller, and Torbjörn Bergman, *Cabinets and Coalition Bargaining: The Democractic Life Cycle in Western Europe* (Oxford: Oxford University Press, 2008).

Thaler, Richard H., and H. M. Shefrin, "An Economic Theory of Self-Control," *Journal of Political Economy* 89, no. 2 (April 1981): 392–406.

The Cabinet Papers, CAB/23/30. June 2, 1922, UK National Archives.

The Cabinet Papers, CAB/23/37. September 2, 1920, UK National Archives.

The Cabinet Papers, CAB/24/122. March 21, 1921, UK National Archives.

The Cabinet Papers, CAB/24/110. July 29, 1920. UK National Archives.

Tolley, H., "The Concealed Crack in the Citadel: The United Nations Commission on Human Rights' Response to Confidential Communications," *Human Rights Quarterly* 6, no. 4 (November 1984): 420–462.

Tolstoy, Leo, *Anna Karenina* (New York: Dover, [1877] 2012).

United Nations, "Report of the Committee against Torture Fifty-third Session (November 3–28, 2014) Fifty-fourth Session (April 20–May 15, 2015)," General Assembly Official Records Seventieth Session Supplement No. 44.

United Nations, "Assessment Mission by the Office of the United Nations High Commissioner for Human Rights to Improve Human Rights, Accountability, Reconciliation and Capacity in South Sudan." Report of the United Nations High Commissioner for Human Rights. A/HRC/31/49 (2016).

United Nations General Assembly, "Report of the Special Rapporteur on Extrajudicial, Summary or Arbitrary Executions," No. A/HRC/11/2/Add.5 (May 28, 2009).

United States Department of Justice. "Nine FIFA Officials and Five Corporate Executives Indicted for Racketeering Conspiracy and Corruption," Department of Justice Office of Public Affairs (May 27, 2015).

United States Department of State, Bureau of Democracy, Human Rights, and Labor, *India Country Reports on Human Rights Practices 2002* (March 31, 2003).

United States Department of State, Bureau of Democracy, Human Rights, and Labor, *2004 Country Reports on Human Rights Practices* (February 25, 2005). http://www.state.gov/j/drl/rls/hrrpt/2004/41720.htm (accessed May 3, 2016).

United States Department of State, Bureau of Democracy, Human Rights, and Labor, *Country Reports on Human Rights Practices for 2015* (2016). http://www.state.gov/j/drl/rls/hrrpt/humanrightsreport/index.htm#wrapper (accessed May 3, 2016).

United States District Court, Southern District of New York, *Sharif Stinson et al., against City of New York.* https://law.justia.com/cases/federal/district-courts/new-york/nysdce/1:2010cv04228/363503/265/ (accessed November 10, 2020).

United States District Court for the Eastern District of Michigan, *United States of America v. Oliver Schmidt* (2016). https://www.justice.gov/opa/press-release/file/923686/download (accessed January 9, 2018).

United States House Committee on Energy and Commerce, 114 Congress (October 8, 2015). http://docs.house.gov/meetings/IF/IF02/20151008/104046/HHRG-114-IF02-Transcript-20151008.pdf.

Wallace, Catriona M., and Geoff Eagleson, "The Sacrificial HR Strategy in Call Centers," *International Journal of Service Industry Management* 11, no. 2 (May 2000): 174–184.

Whillans, Ashley V., Elizabeth W. Dunn, Paul Smeets, Rene Bekkers, and Michael I. Norton, "Buying Time Promotes Happiness," *Proceedings of the National Academy of Sciences* 144, no. 32 (August 2017). http://www.pnas.org/content/early/2017/07/18/1706541114.full (accessed July 27, 2017).

Williamson, Oliver E., "Transaction-Cost Economics: The Governance of Contractual Relations," *Journal of Law and Economics* 22, no. 2 (March 1979): 233–261.

Williamson, Oliver E., "Opportunism and Its Critics," *Managerial and Decision Economics* 14, no. 2 (March/April 1993): 97–107.

Williamson, Oliver E., "Public and Private Bureaucracies: A Transaction Cost Economics Perspective," *The Journal of Law, Economics, and Organization* 15, no. 1 (March 1999): 306–342.

Wilson, James Q., *Bureaucracy* (New York: Basic Books, 1989).

Wood, Elisabeth, "Armed Groups and Sexual Violence: When Is Wartime Rape Rare," *Politics and Society* 37, no. 1 (March 2009): 131–162.

Wood, Elisabeth, "Rape as a Practice of War: Toward a Typology of Political Violence," *Politics and Society* 46, no. 4 (December 2018): 513–537.

Woodcock, Jamie, *Working the Phones Control and Resistance in Call Centres* (London: Pluto Press, 2017).

Index

For the benefit of digital users, indexed terms that span two pages (e.g., 52–53) may, on occasion, appear on only one of those pages.

Tables and figures are indicated by *t* and *f* following the page number

Printed in the USA/Agawam, MA
April 21, 2021

773445.009